BOREDOM BUSTER

ACKNOWLEDGEMENTS

Publishing Director	Piers Pickard
Publisher	Tim Cook
Commissioning Editor	Jen Feroze
Author	Nicola Baxter
Designer	Andy Mansfield
Americanization	Jennifer Dixon
Print production	Larissa Frost,
	Nigel Longuet

Lonely Planet Offices

Australia

Level 2 and 3, 551 Swanston Street, Carlton 3053, Victoria, Australia
Phone: 03 8379 8000 Email: talk2us@lonelyplanet.com.au

USA

150 Linden St, Oakland, CA 94607
Phone: 510 250 6400 Email: info@lonelyplanet.com

United Kingdom

240 Blackfriars Road, London, SE1 8NW
Phone: 020 3771 5100 Email: go@lonelyplanet.co.uk

Published in April 2016 by Lonely Planet Publications Pty Ltd
ABN 36 005 607 983
ISBN 978 1 76034 106 0
www.lonelyplanetkids.com
© Lonely Planet 2016
Printed in China

10 9 8 7 6 5 4 3 2 1

MIX
Paper from
responsible sources
FSC™ C021741

Paper in this book is certified against the
Forest Stewardship Council™ standards.
FSC™ promotes environmentally responsible,
socially beneficial and economically viable
management of the world's forests.

FLIP OF THE DICE!

How cool is this? If you want
to play a game needing dice,
this book will magically turn
into one. All you have to do
is shut your eyes and flip the
left-hand pages towards the
front from wherever you are
in the book. Stop at random.
Whatever you see at the
top left of the page is your
"throw."

Practice to make sure you can
do it smoothly.
Good luck!

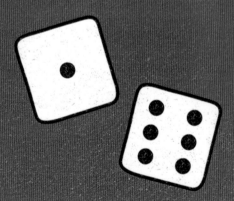

HOW TO BUST THAT BOREDOM

BE PREPARED...

...for anything! When you're on the move, it's wise to expect the unexpected. You may whizz straight to your destination or get stuck in a traffic jam. Flights can be delayed and bags go astray.

If you have emergency supplies with you, holdups can be part of the adventure. That means a little money, food and drink, a change of clothes, and something to pass the time. This Boredom Buster is the perfect travel pal!

THE SECRET...

...of awesome boredom busting is plenty of variety. You'll find dozens of different games, challenges, and activities in these pages. Some are more fun if the whole family joins in. Some are just for you when you want a bit of peace and quiet. You might even be inspired to invent some games of your own.

You don't need to write in the book, but there are a couple of places where folding the page will add to the fun.

YOU'LL NEED...

...not much, really. Pens, pencils, and paper are always handy, but you don't need them to have fun with the Boredom Buster. Counters for games are helpful, though, but you don't need anything special for these. Some not-too-sticky candies or small coins will do the trick. Scrunched-up candy wrappers, especially foil ones, make good counters, too, and can even double as a mini tennis ball (see page 36) or soccer ball (page 55)!

A watch or cell phone is handy for timing yourself, or you can ask a travel buddy to do this instead.

CONTENTS

I SPY

You know how this goes... One person says, "I spy with my little eye..." and gives a clue to something they have spotted. Everyone else has to guess what it is. Here are some clues to choose.

THE CLASSIC

"I spy with my little eye something beginning with B!" (or any other letter). If you're playing with little brothers or sisters, you could say, "...something that starts with a *buh* sound."

THE CUNNING

"I spy with my little eye something beginning with ARC!" Add more letters and you'll get some wild suggestions. A ridiculous child? All round coins? A racing car?

THE RAINBOW

"I spy with my little eye something that's BLUE!" You can keep the colors simple or show off your inner artist. Chartreuse, magenta, or taupe anyone?

THE POETIC

"I spy with my little eye something that rhymes with STAR!" Car? Tar? Jar? Bar? Bra? Haha!

THE TEASE

"I spy with my little eye something that can wave!" A hand? A flag? A tree branch? Er ... the sea? These clues can be truly tricky!

TOP TIP

Players have to be able to spy what YOU spy. Don't choose the cat on a wall that you passed ten minutes ago or the candy you just scoffed.

MEMORY TEST

You can play this by yourself, but it's more fun (and not so easy to cheat) with someone else.
Look at the page for exactly one minute. Then close the book or pass it to your travel buddy.
How many of the ten items can you remember? Page 126 rates your score.

CAN YOU...

We're all different. It doesn't matter in the least if you and your friends can do any of the random things below or not, but it's fun to find out.

...RAISE ONE EYEBROW?

And if so, can you raise (just) the other one, too? Cool, if you're thinking of playing James Bond. Not much use otherwise.

...ROLL YOUR TONGUE?

You know ... curl up the edges so it looks like a tube. No one quite knows why some people can do this and others can't. Even twins can be different.

...KEEP GOING CLOCKWISE?

Lift one foot off the ground and start drawing a circle in the air in a clockwise direction with your foot. Now draw a six (6) in the air with your finger. Does your foot change direction?

...RUB AND PAT?

Can you pat your head with one hand and rub your stomach, going around and around, with the other hand?

...NOT BE A MIRROR?

Draw circles in the air with your two index fingers, so that both fingers are going clockwise. Start slowly, then get faster and faster. What happens?

...WIGGLE YOUR EARS?

Apparently, if, like most people, you can't do this, you can learn to. But, well, WHY?

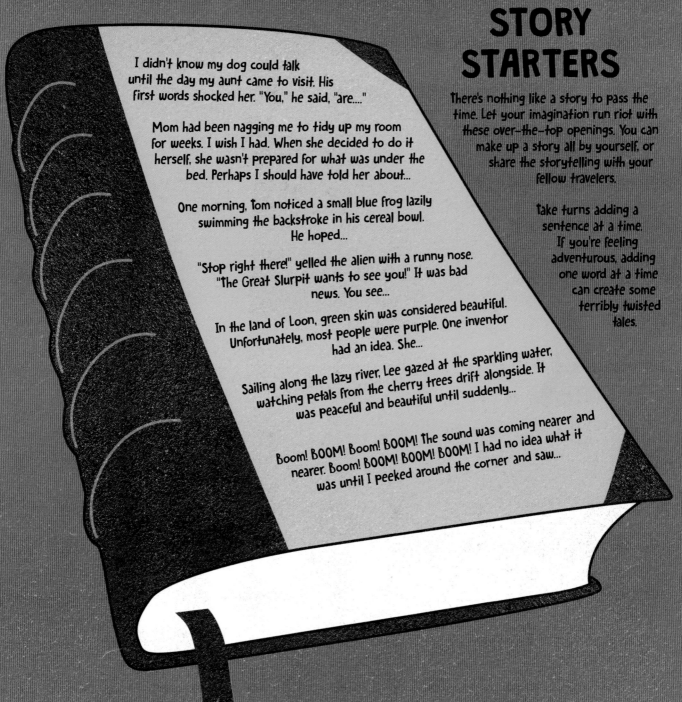

STORY STARTERS

I didn't know my dog could talk until the day my aunt came to visit. His first words shocked her. "You," he said, "are...."

Mom had been nagging me to tidy up my room for weeks. I wish I had. When she decided to do it herself, she wasn't prepared for what was under the bed. Perhaps I should have told her about...

One morning, Tom noticed a small blue frog lazily swimming the backstroke in his cereal bowl. He hoped...

"Stop right there!" yelled the alien with a runny nose. "The Great Slurpit wants to see you!" It was bad news. You see...

In the land of Loon, green skin was considered beautiful. Unfortunately, most people were purple. One inventor had an idea. She...

Sailing along the lazy river, Lee gazed at the sparkling water, watching petals from the cherry trees drift alongside. It was peaceful and beautiful until suddenly...

Boom! BOOM! Boom! BOOM! The sound was coming nearer and nearer. Boom! BOOM! BOOM! BOOM! I had no idea what it was until I peeked around the corner and saw...

There's nothing like a story to pass the time. Let your imagination run riot with these over-the-top openings. You can make up a story all by yourself, or share the storytelling with your fellow travelers.

Take turns adding a sentence at a time. If you're feeling adventurous, adding one word at a time can create some terribly twisted tales.

9

PUZZLING PLACES

Sort out these mixed-up cities, countries, and continents. The clues may make your sorting speedier. Page 126 has the answers.

YUKERT
Part of Europe and Asia, is it a country or a bird?

WORN KEY
City often known as the Big Apple

SUSAIR
The largest country in the world

NOODLN
Big Ben and Beefeaters in western Europe

ECOMIX
Aztec ruins and tasty tacos in the Americas

HANCI
Country with the biggest population in the world

KOOTY
Asian capital city with great sushi

ROGASNIPE
Southeast Asian city-state where chewing gum is banned

ZIBLAR
Home to a huge South American rainforest

PLANE
Asian country with the world's highest mountain

CRAFEN
European country known for fashion and food

CANTATRICA
The coldest, driest, and windiest continent of them all

NERDANGLE
The biggest island in the world

RATALUSIA
Down under or up over? It depends where you are!

GETPY
Pyramids and palm trees in north Africa

HOW MANY CANDIES IN THE JAR?

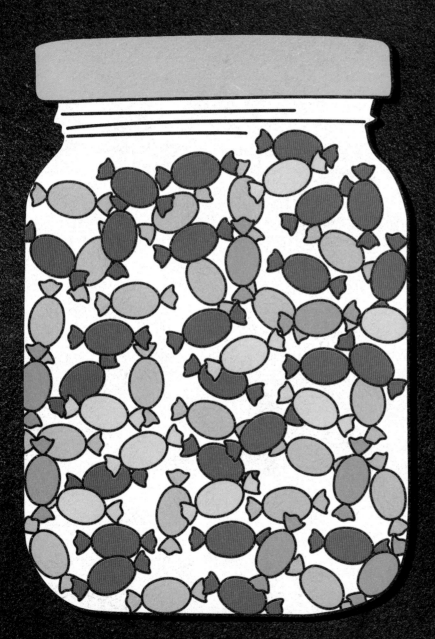

How good is your guesstimating? Don't count these candies but show them to your travel buddies and guess how many goodies are in the jar. The winner is the closest to the correct answer, which is on page 126.

Make sure no one has more than ten seconds to look at the picture.

MORSE CODE

This code was invented in the 1800s to send messages by telegraph, using clicking sounds. Now we have texting and messaging and lots of ways of keeping in touch, but Morse is still a cool code for secrets.

A . _
B _ . . .
C _ . _ .
D _ . .
E .
F . . _ .
G _ _ .
H . . . .
I . .
J . _ _ _
K _ . _
L . _ . .
M _ _

N _ .
O _ _ _
P . _ _ .
Q _ _ . _
R . _ .
S . . .
T _
U . . _
V . . . _
W . _ _
X _ . . _
Y _ . _ _
Z _ _ . .

The good thing about this code is all the different ways you can send it.

SOUNDS
Tapping, humming, clapping, singing, finger-snapping, snorting ... whatever! Remember to leave a space between each letter and a longer space between each word.

LIGHTS
Great for important messages at night. Try short and long flashes with a flashlight or phone light.

SHAPES
Choose one shape for dots and one for dashes.

COLORS
Yep, you guessed it ... one color for dots and one for dashes, then use any shapes you want. Dots, stripes, stars?

EXTRA CUNNING
Use capital letters for dashes and small letters for dots. The letters can say anything you want. It's the hidden Morse message that counts.

CRACK THE CODES

Now you know about Morse code, try to figure out what the messages below say.
Then write, tap, cough, or draw some messages of your own.

· — · · — · ·   · — — ·

— · · · · — · · — · · — — · · —

ΦOΦO ΦΦΦ ΦΦ O   Φ ΦΦΦ   ΦΦ ΦOΦΦ
OΦΦO OΦ OΦO Φ ΦOΦΦ
ΦΦΦ ΦO   ΦΦ ΦΦΦ ΦO ΦOO OΦ ΦOΦΦ

WA l r U   SE s   aR E   VE ry Coo La nd SOa reyo U

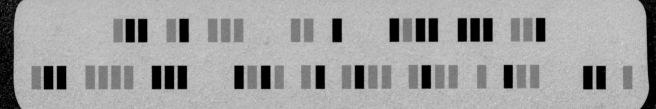

13

BING, BEEP, BUZZ!

This game can go on for hours. In fact, it's best when everyone has totally forgotten about it and one person loudly remembers!

1. Each person chooses a noise that they can shout out quickly and loudly.

BANG!

2. Someone chooses a slightly rare item you might see along the way. A yellow car? A man with an umbrella? A church flying a flag? A tandem bicycle? A car just like yours?

3. The first person to spot the object shouts out their word. If they're right, they get a point and choose the next item.

POW!

4. No points if you get too excited and shout someone else's word or have long ago forgotten the item and shout out an earlier one.

ZAP!

PING!

TONGUE TWISTERS

Can you get your tongue, teeth, and the rest of your face around these tortuous twisters?
Practice makes perfect, they say, but you may drive your friends mad in the meantime.

Greek grapes, Greek grapes,
Greek grapes...

How much wood would
a woodchuck chuck if a
woodchuck could chuck wood?

Roberta ran rings around the
Roman ruins.

Red leather, yellow leather, red
leather, yellow leather...

Wayne went to Wales to
watch walruses.

She sells seashells on
the seashore...

Peter Piper picked a peck of pickled peppers.
A peck of pickled peppers Peter Piper picked.
If Peter Piper picked a peck of pickled peppers,
Where's the peck of pickled peppers Peter Piper picked?

Whether the weather is warm,
whether the weather is hot,
we have to put up with the weather,
whether we like it or not.

Toy boat, toy boat, toy boat...

If two witches watch two
watches, which witch watches
which watch?

I scream, You scream, We all
scream for ice cream...

HOW MANY TRIANGLES?

How many triangles can you see? Check page 126 to see if you missed any.

MIND READING

If you know how this trick works already, try it on your travel buddies.
If not, follow the steps below, and all will be revealed!

Slowly and mysteriously, tell your pal:

1. I want you to think of a number under 10.
Don't tell me what it is!

2. Add 5 to it.

3. Double what you now have.

4. Subtract 6.

5. Half it.

6. Subtract the number you first
thought of.

Now look into my eyes. Think hard
about the number you have left ... let me
concentrate ... I can read your mind ...
the number you have left is ... 2!

When you try this on your friends, you don't ever need to know
their mystery number. You just need to make sure that you
remember how much you added to it or subtracted from it, and
if you multiplied it, remember to divide it again before the end.

So in this one, you added 5 to x (the mystery number), so you
had x plus 5. Then you doubled it, so you had 2 of x plus 10.
Then you subtracted 6, so you had 2 of x plus 4. Then you halved
it, leaving just x and 2. So when you took away x (whatever that
was!), you ended up with 2.

If you keep track of them, you can include as many stages as
you want, so your friend will be even more mystified.

ROCK, PAPER, SCISSORS

This is a good game that needs no equipment – just your hands.
You can have a contest or use it to decide who goes first in a game.

1. Face your opponent. Clench one fist and raise it up and down, saying together, "One, two, three..."

2. Instead of "four!" you show each other one of three hand shapes.
It's important to do this at exactly the same time.

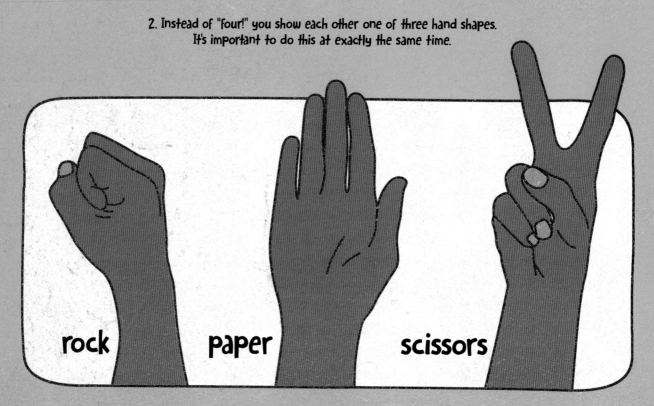

rock   paper   scissors

3. You need to know that paper wraps up rock (so paper wins).
Scissors cut paper (so scissors wins).
Rock blunts scissors (so rock wins).

In other words, scissors beats paper but loses to rock.
Rock beats scissors but loses to paper.
Paper beats rock but loses to scissors.

If you both make the same shape, it's a tie and you do it again.

DOWNTIME DREAMS

When you want a quiet couple of minutes, gently follow the path below with your finger. Each time you come to a loop, stop and think about someone you really like. Imagine their face, their voice, their smile. Then go on and "meet" someone else at the next loop. You'll see that some people can make you smile even when they're not with you!

CHECKERS

This game for two has been played for hundreds – maybe thousands – of years.
If your journey feels almost as long, try this game. It's easy, but there's plenty of skill involved.

Each player needs 12 playing pieces of their own color. Coins are good. They don't need to be all of the same value, as long as one player has copper-colored coins and the other has silver-colored ones.

1. Each player puts their pieces on the board on the black spaces nearest them. Pieces never go on the white spaces in this game. They always move diagonally from black square to black square.

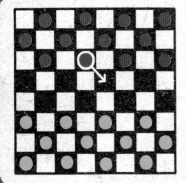

2. The darkest color always starts. Players take turns moving one piece to the next black square. You can only move forwards, towards your opponent. No retreating!

3. If your next move takes you to an opponent's piece and there is a black space beyond it, you must jump over the piece and take it off the board. You have to do it, even if that means next time your opponent can jump over your piece and remove it. When you have jumped over a piece, if there is another piece and another space, you can keep jumping and taking the pieces until you have to stop.

4. If one of your pieces reaches the far side of the board, it becomes a king and is "crowned" by putting one of your pieces that has already been taken on top of it. A king is a very powerful piece, because it can go backwards as well as forwards. Kings can jump over and take pieces, but take care ... ordinary pieces can take them, as well.

5. The winner is the person who takes all the other player's pieces or makes it impossible for them to move.

PLAYER ONE

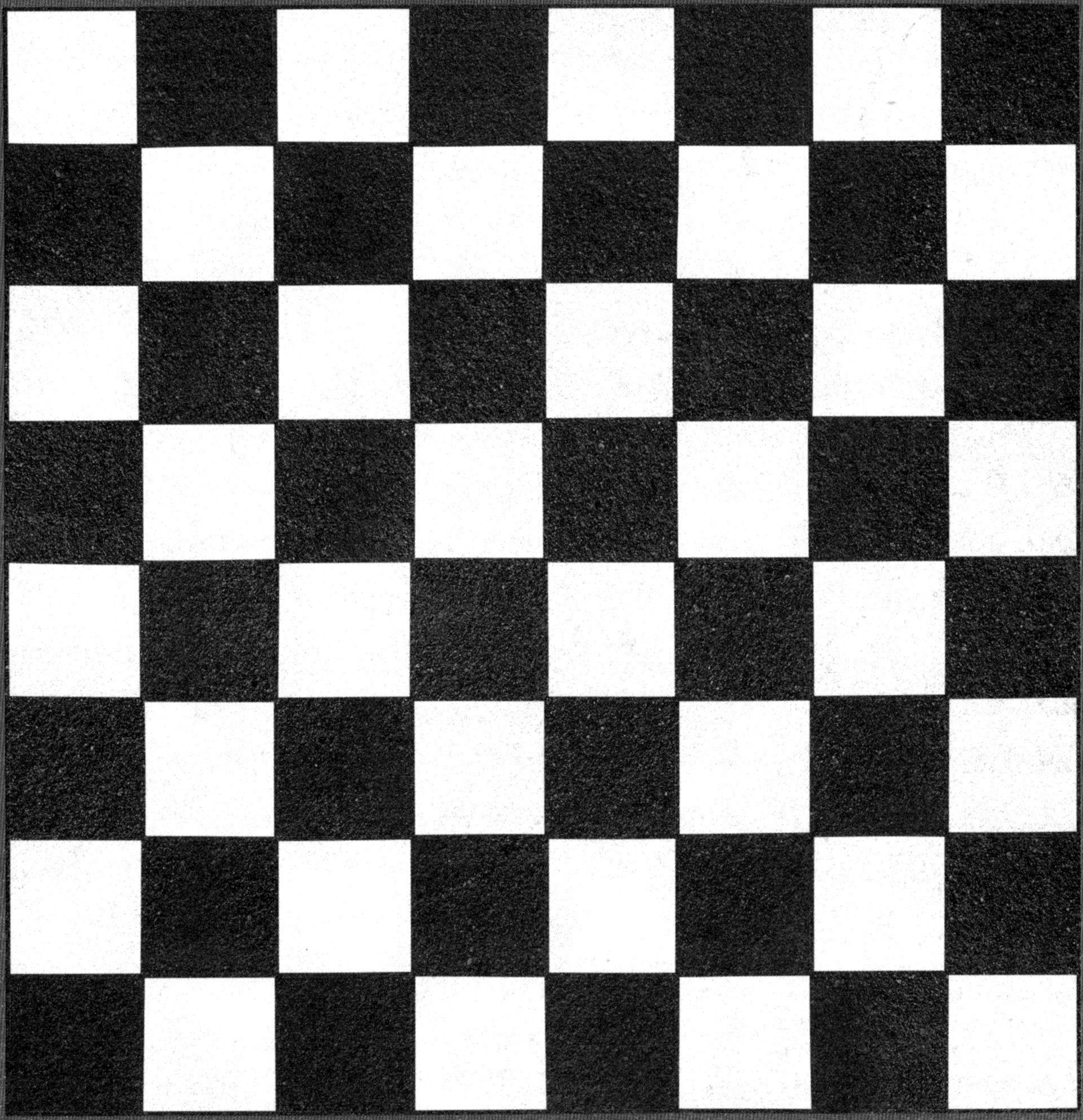

PLAYER TWO

ROAD—TRIP BINGO

Grab some coins or candies to cover the pictures as you
spot these items on your journey. You can play by yourself or in competition
with someone else on the opposite page. Decide if the winner is the first
to complete a row, a column, or the whole board.

fir tree		pick-up truck		movie theater	
	animal road sign		worker in a hard hat		church with a spire
detour sign		dog on a leash		gas station	
	traffic lights		pink car		sheep
flag flying		cat		horse	
	police car		airplane		tractor

Some bingo players shout "HOUSE!" when they have filled their card. That seems wrong if you're traveling. How about "CAR!" or "TRUCK!" or "BUS!" instead? Take your pick!

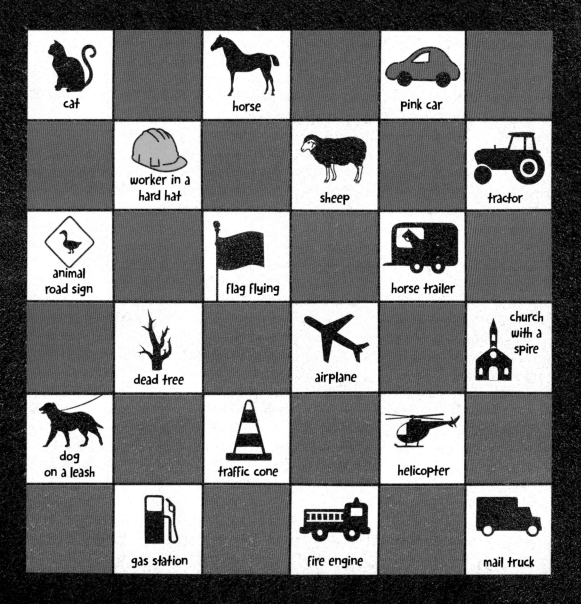

cat		horse		pink car	
	worker in a hard hat		sheep		tractor
animal road sign		flag flying		horse trailer	
	dead tree		airplane		church with a spire
dog on a leash		traffic cone		helicopter	
	gas station		fire engine		mail truck

TRAVEL TEASERS

Can you figure out these roaming riddles?
Answers are on page 126 if you get stuck.

1 Two mothers and two grown-up daughters went on a trip together but they only needed to buy three tickets. Why?

2 As I was going to St. Ives,
I met a man with seven wives.
Each wife had seven sacks,
Each sack had seven cats,
Each cat had seven kittens,
Kittens, cats, sacks, and wives,
How many were going to St. Ives?

3 What can travel around the world by staying in the corner?

4 Ben went on vacation. He arrived at the campsite on Friday and stayed for four nights. He left again on Friday. How?

OPTICAL ILLUSIONS

Drivers and pilots need to have their wits about them, whether they are squeezing into a parking space or landing on a narrow runway. But can you always believe what your eyes see? Try these tricks to find out how eagle-eyed you are. Page 126 gives you the answers.

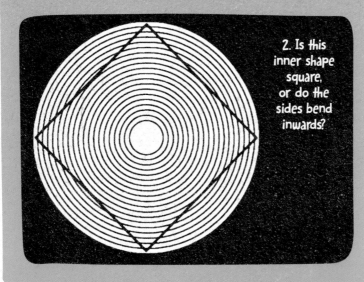

2. Is this inner shape square, or do the sides bend inwards?

3. Which of the two short lines is longest?

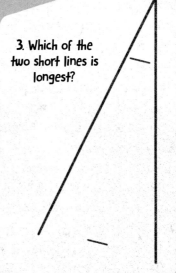

1. Which is taller? The top two triangles or the gap between them and the one at the bottom?

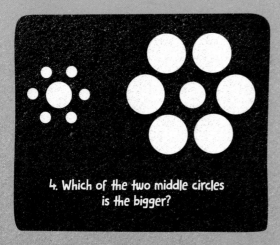

4. Which of the two middle circles is the bigger?

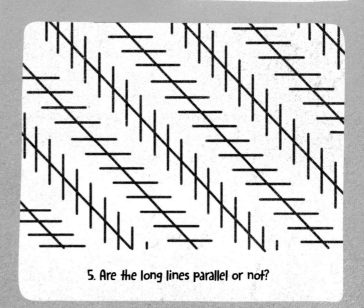

5. Are the long lines parallel or not?

CLICK, CLAP, BOOM!

Let's face it, not everyone is a great singer, but most people have got clapping, slapping, or snapping down to a fine art. Try this fun game.

All you have to do is to tap, clap, or click the rhythm of a well-known tune. It can be a nursery rhyme, a pop song, the theme tune from a TV program – anything that usually has a tune but in your version doesn't.

Your travel buddies' job is to guess that tune. It should be easy, right?

Actually, with some tunes, it is. Do you know this?

Diddle-dum, diddle-dum, diddle-dum-dum-DUM!
Diddle-dum, diddle-dum, diddle-dum-dum-DUM!
Diddle-dum, diddle-dum, diddle-dum-dum-dum!
Diddle-duuuuum, dum-diddle, dum, dum, dum.

With others, it's a lot trickier. This is a well-known nursery rhyme:

Dum, dum, dum, dum, da, da, dum,
Da, da, da, da, dum.
Da, dum, dum, dum, da, dum, dum, dum,
Da, da, da, da, dum.
Diddle-da, da, dum, diddle-da, da, dum,
Diddle-dum, diddle-dum, diddle-diddle- dum-dum,
Dum, dum, dum, dum, da, da, dum,
Da, da, da, da, dum.

Any ideas? Think farming or look at page 126. Now try for yourself!

ALL ANIMALS

Here are two easy games about animals. Remember, you don't need to be able to see real live animals to play, though they count as well. Animals on road signs, shop signs, trucks, or billboards are fine, too.

MOO, BAA, OINK!

Every time anyone sees an animal, they have to make a sound just like it. The last one to do so is out. Sounds easy? What noise are you going to make if you see a giraffe?

ANIMAL STARS

Divide into two teams. Each team is on the lookout for animals and scores one point for each one seen. If you're speeding past a herd of cows, you can only add as many as you can count as you go past. Decide between you if you're going to count birds as well, or just four-footed friends.

The team with the most points at an agreed time is the winner.

HOW MANY BUTTERFLIES?

How many butterflies have fluttered by here? Don't count them. Use your great guesstimating skills. Give yourself and your friends just ten seconds each to look at the picture, then give your guesses. Which of you is closest? Find out on page 126.

SECRET LANGUAGES

Sometimes you just can't get away from everyone to pass on a top-secret message. Try one of these tried and tested languages instead. They may take a bit of practice, but they'll be useful in all sorts of ways. Just don't show this book to you-know-who...

1. One of the easiest to learn, this language is often called Pig Latin. All you do is move the beginning of the word to the end and add "-ay." So, "We're going on a trip" would be "E'reway oingay noay a-ay iptray."

2. Called Obby Dobby or Ob, this one is also simple but strange. If a word starts with a vowel, put "ob" at the beginning. If it starts with a consonant, put "ob" after the consonant and after every other consonant that begins a syllable. So "We take off tomorrow" would be "W-ob-e tob-ake ob-off t-ob-mob-o-rob-ow."

3. Eggy Peggy works by adding "egg" before each vowel. So "How long before we get there?" would become "Heggow leggong beggefeggore wegge gegget theggere?"

Lohelay!

Hobeloblobo!

Heggelleggo!

ALPHABET TRIP

Sometimes travelers have to be inventive! Play the game below with as many friends as you want. You'll need a good memory and some strange ways of getting from A to B (or A to Z, in fact!).

First player: On my way to Bulawayo (or any other place you care to name), I traveled in an Airplane.

Next player: On my way to Bulawayo, I traveled in an Airplane and a Boat and on a Camel.

A B C D E F G H I J K L M N

Next player: On my way to Bulawayo, I traveled in an Airplane and a Boat.

T

C

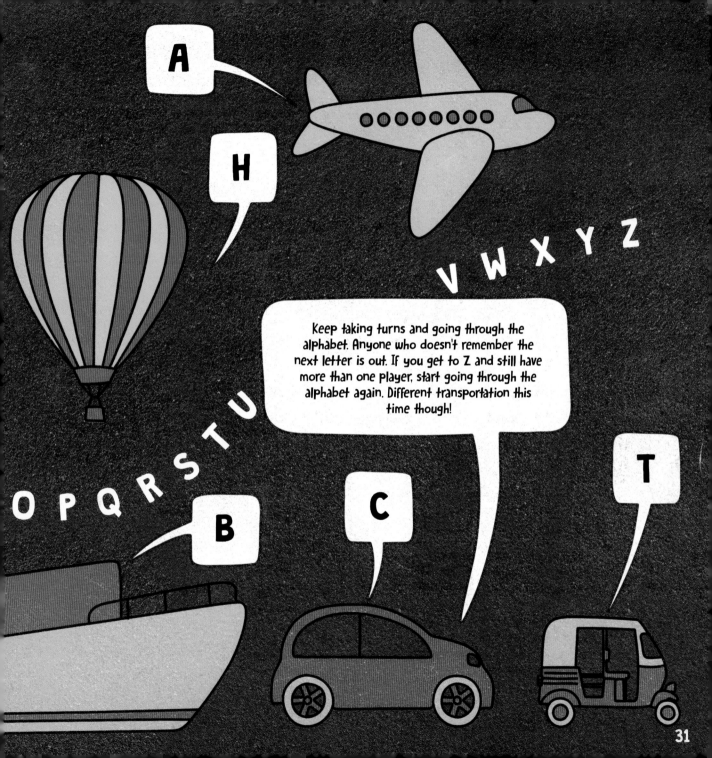

31

''HO AM I?

All these games start with one player choosing a character known to the other players. It could be someone famous or their nearest and dearest. Then the other players try to guess who they are thinking of.

Try all these variations to find your favorite.

? THREE CLUES

Just think of three things that strike you about the person and boldly announce them. "I am a bit bald. I wear glasses. I am very tall."

It's up to the others to guess. No questions. If they get really stuck, give them an extra clue.

? IMPRESSIONS

This is one for the actors among you. Other players can ask you any questions they want, but you have to answer as if you were the secret person. Imitate the voice and the mannerisms.

More points for you the quicker you're guessed!

? 20 QUESTIONS

Players have only 20 questions between them to guess who you are. Keep score to make sure they don't ask 40 questions!

You can only answer "yes" or "no." So "What color is your hair?" won't work, but "Are you blonde?" will.

HOW MANY RECTANGLES?

Can you count the rectangles in this picture? There are lots more than you might think at first.
Squares are a kind of rectangle, so you can count those as well.
Turn to page 126 to see if you found them all.

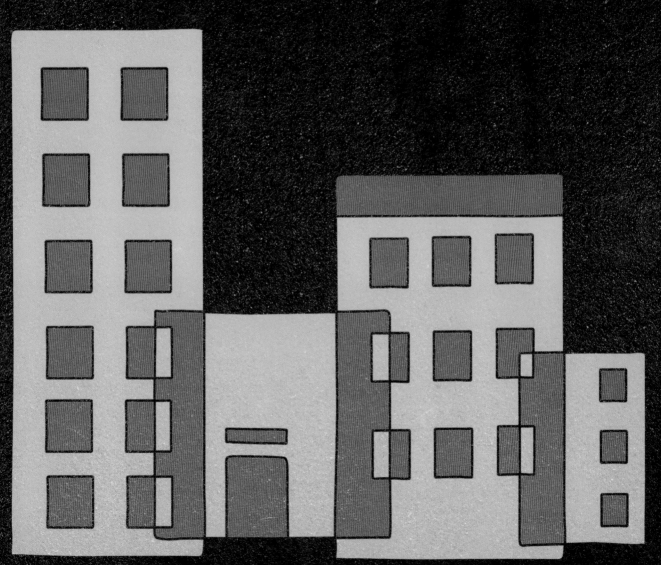

FIZZ, BUZZ!

This is a game that can be played anywhere by any number of players. The faster you play, the harder and funnier it gets. Numbers will never seem the same again!

The rules are very simple. You have to start counting at one and take turns saying the next number.

The only tricky thing is that every time you come to a number that can be divided by three, instead of the number, you say FIZZ!

And every time you come to a number that can be divided by seven, instead of the number, you say BUZZ!

And if you come to a number that can be divided by three and seven? FIZZ! BUZZ!

So you will start like this:
One, two, FIZZ!, four, five, FIZZ!, BUZZ!, eight, FIZZ!, ten...

FOR LITTLES...

If little brothers and sisters are playing, you can say FIZZ! and BUZZ! when the number itself has a three or a seven in it. So 17 would be BUZZ! and 37 would be FIZZ! BUZZ!

FOR BIGS...

Just in case your parents get annoyingly good at this, change the numbers each time to any two between one and ten. Warning: Don't choose one!

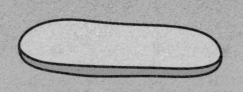

MYSTERY BAG

Ask an adult to secretly gather a few small items and put one of them in a plastic shopping bag or under a coat or rug.

One person has to feel in the bag or under the coat or rug and silently guess what it is they are holding.

Then they have to describe exactly what they feel to other players. Everyone has a guess about what the object is. Those who guess correctly gain a point. The player feeling and describing also gets a point for every other person who gets it right. Then the next person plays with a new object.

The winner is the person with the most points at the end.

SWEET SECRETS

This is a crazy game, but good fun. You need a bag of candies that are all the same shape but different flavors. With eyes shut, the player takes a piece of candy. Before they open their eyes, they have to first smell the candy and guess the flavor, and then put it into their mouth and guess the flavor or the color.

−2

3

2

3

−2

FLICK TENNIS

Anyone for tennis?

This is not a page, it's a tennis net! At least, the other side of it is.

This is a game for two players.

You need to fold the page in half along the dotted line to make a net across the court on pages 36 and 39.

Scrunch up a small piece of paper, such as a candy wrapper, and use it as a tennis ball.

The players take turns balancing the ball on their thumbnail and flicking it across the net. They get points as shown on the court for where it lands. No points at all if it misses the court completely and two points taken from their score if it lands between the lines on the sides of the court.

The first to ten points wins the game.
The winner of six games wins the set.
The winner of two sets wins the match.

Good luck!

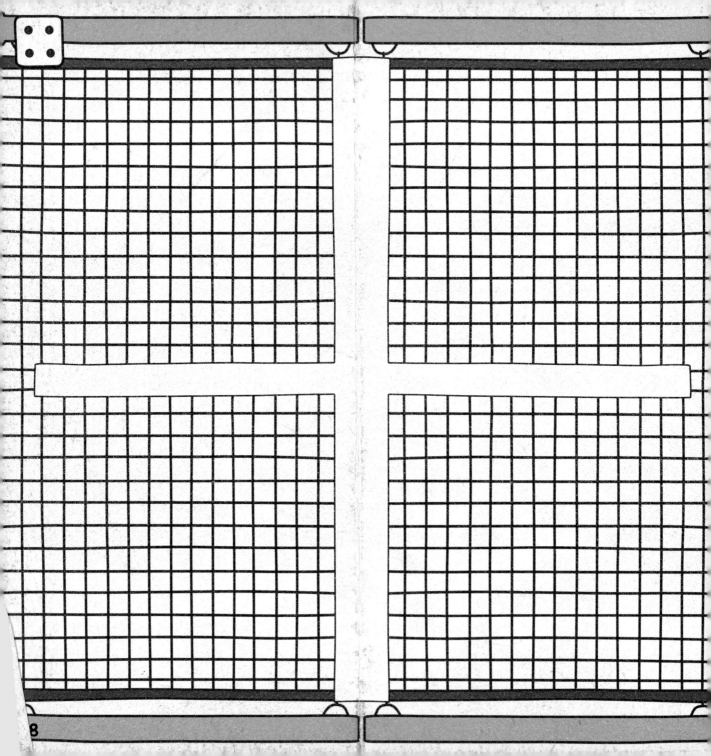

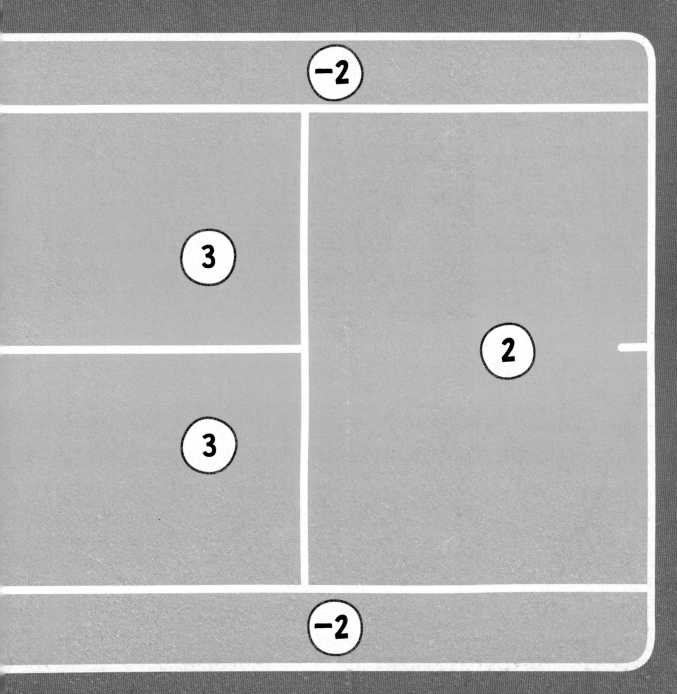

39

RADIO GAMES

If you're in a car and have a radio or CD player, or a phone or other way of playing music, try these noisy games.

NAME THAT TUNE

Turn on the radio to a music station. (Find one where there is music playing right now!) The first person to shout out the name of the song that is playing is the winner.

NAME THAT ARTIST

Play as for NAME THAT TUNE, but this time the winner is the first to correctly name the singer or band.

WORD BINGO

Each player chooses a word of four or more letters. The radio is turned on to a music or talk station. The player whose word is first heard is the winner of that round. It's best to change stations for each round, so it's harder to guess what might be said or sung.

SING ALONG SONG

Use the radio or a music player for this. Put on a well-known song that everyone can sing along to. Then turn down the sound and let one brave player or a group of you sing on. After a verse or two, turn up the sound again and find out how far off the original you are! Being close to the recording gets you cheers and applause. Being far off gets you groans and boos.

KEYS, PLEASE

Car keys, suitcase keys, hotel room keys — it's good to keep an eye on them when you're traveling, and having more than one copy is a top travel tip. These keys all have a twin except one. Can you find which it is? Check your answer on page 126.

ALTER EGOS

Use these tables to create new identities for you and your travel buddies, and read each of your selections aloud. Each of you must now become these characters. The first person to slip up and use their real name or real voice is out.

The name's Savage. Hunter Savage.

Hi, my name is Kay Griffin.

Find the first letter of your first name in this table. This is your new first name.

A – Star	H – Bailey	O – Frankie	V – Robin
B – Spike	I – Jesse	P – Logan	W – Blake
C – Lucky	J – Scout	Q – River	X – Drew
D – Skye	K – Zane	R – Harper	Y – Jordan
E – Avery	L – Cameron	S – Morgan	Z – Kay
F – Hunter	M – Ash	T – Alex	
G – Taylor	N – Charlie	U – Shannon	

Frankie Fox is the name.

Hi, my name is Star Love.

Find your birth month in this table. This is your new last name.

January – Speed	July – Love
February – Summers	August – Havoc
March – Kent	September – Knight
April – Griffin	October – Valentine
May – Savage	November – Diamond
June – Fox	December – Black

Hi, my name is River Black.

Jesse Diamond at your service.

I have to
SHOUT
one word
every time
I speak.

Shhh! I can only speak
very, very quietly!

So, like, my
new identity
is really, like,
cool.

Find your birth date in this table.
This is the way your new identity speaks.
Good luck!

1 – Speak in a high and squeaky voice
2 – Clear your throat at the end of every sentence
3 – Cover your mouth with your hand when you speak
4 – Don't speak louder than a whisper
5 – Speak in a singsong voice
6 – Shout one word in every sentence
7 – Keep one eye shut when you speak
8 – Say "like" at least twice in every sentence
9 – Be really overdramatic
10 – Phrase everything you say as if it's a question
11 – Hold your nose when you speak
12 – Quack like a duck at the start of every sentence
13 – Stare at whoever you're talking to without blinking
14 – Laugh out loud after anyone else finishes speaking
15 – Speak like a robot
16 – Stick your tongue out while you're speaking
17 – Open your mouth extra wide when you talk
18 – Use extra long words whenever you can
19 – Speak really slooooowly
20 – Make your voice really deep
21 – Speak as if you're introducing a movie
22 – Speak for as long as you can without taking a breath
23 – Make every word in a sentence start with the same letter
24 – You're not allowed to use the words "err" or "um"
25 – Keep a giant grin fixed on your face when you speak
26 – Hum a little tune at the end of each sentence
27 – Say everything as fast as you possibly can
28 – No words for you! Communicate using actions only
29 – Constantly interrupt your travel buddies
30 – Say all your sentences backwards
31 – Pretend to be another person on your trip when you speak

It is such a
lovely day,
isn't it?

Look!
Large
lions
licking
lollipops!

This is
stupendously
fantastical.

BALLOON ESCAPE

A bunch of 50 balloons ... a sudden gust of wind ... oops! In ten seconds, guesstimate how many balloons are floating into the blue. Does the unlucky balloon-buyer have any left at all? Turn to page 126 to see if you're right.

DREAM DESTINATIONS

If you're desperate to start exploring but you're stuck in a car, plane, or train, set out anyway ... in your head! Follow the track with your finger. When you come to a star, stop and think of a place you'd really like to visit. Imagine the sights, sounds, and even the smells of your stopover, then move along to the next one.
You can travel the world in secret style!

PLACE–NAME PUZZLES

All these games are about place names, but it doesn't matter if they are countries, cities, rivers, towns, villages, or even streets.

END TO END

How many place names can you think of that begin and end with the same letter, such as Asia, Alabama, or Warsaw?

NAME NAMES

How many place names can you think of that are a first name? For example, Adelaide or Victoria?

If you include places that have a first name as part of their name, you'll find even more, such as Charleston and Maryland.

And there are lots more that have the same name as someone's surname, such as Wellington, Raleigh, and Livingstone.

SOLO VOWELS

How many place names can you think of that have only one kind of vowel in them. For example, there are Morocco, London, and Mississippi. To count, the place name must have at least two of those same vowels.

PLACE CHAINS

Take turns naming a place, so that each one begins with the last letter of the name before. For example, if someone says "Nigeria," the next person could say "Arkansas" and the next "Sweden."

ROAD SIGNS

Each player chooses one position on a road sign. They might take the first place name, or the second place name, or the bottom place name. Signs with only one place name should be ignored.

Each time they see a road sign, the players add up the number of letters in the name of the place in the position they have chosen. So if they have chosen the first place, and this happens to be Cape Town, they score eight points. The winner is the first to reach 100 points.

SILLY SENTENCES

All you have to do is to make up a senseless sentence where each word starts with a letter from the place name. So PARIS might become Penguins Are Red In Summer and MADRID could be Most Animals Don't Rap In Dreams.

CHOOSE CLUES

In this simple game, each player describes a place name in different words, and the other players have to guess what it is. So someone might say, "Serenade an animal's foot" and the answer could be "Singapore" (Sing-a-paw)!

TWENTY–SEVEN WHAT?

Sometimes this game is very hard to guess.

One player decides on a certain thing they can see outside the car, train, or bus. They don't tell anyone what it is but they start counting out loud every time they see another one. It could be someone wearing a hat, for example, or a car with a luggage rack on top.

Everyone else has to guess what it is the player is counting.

Whoever guesses correctly gets the next chance to choose something.

In order to give everyone a fair chance, it's important to choose something that is seen fairly often. If no counting has been heard for five minutes or a certain distance, the next player starts their turn.

22

35

12

6

1

9

3

5

22

43

15

8 13 79 10

THE NUMBER COLLECTORS

Another good game involving numbers is simply to "collect" them.

You start at one and in order to "collect" this number, you have to see it somewhere – on a car license plate, on a bus, on a road sign. But it has to be a one by itself. It's no good seeing 17 and collecting just the one. Then you just keep counting, each time looking for the next number.

Decide if you will work alone or if all of you traveling will work as a group. You may think that it will be hard to find, say, 173 somewhere, but sooner or later you will spot it and start looking for 174.

This game really can go on forever, and it's so much fun that lots of players can't stop even when they get home!

1 4

3 36

2 14 18 7

NINE MEN'S MORRIS

This is an ancient game that is easy to learn but not easy to win!

You need two players. Each of them has nine "men." Coins or candies would be fine for this, as long as each player has a different color.

Players aim to make "mills," which are three men in a row. The winner is the person whose opponent only has two men left, making it impossible to make a mill.

There are three parts to the game.

1. Place the men. Players start with an empty board and take turns putting a man on one of the blue dots. If they manage to make a mill by doing this, they can take off one of the other player's men, which then doesn't come back into the game. They can take off any man but must choose one not in a mill if possible.

2. When all the men are placed, players take turns moving their men. They can only move one space along the lines to an empty spot each time. No jumping is allowed. They are still trying to make mills and so take off one of their opponent's men.

A player is allowed to make a mill, move one man, then make the same mill again – over and over again. Clever players get into a position where by moving one man they can make a mill at every turn. It is hard for the other player to win if they are losing a man at every play.

3. As soon as a player has only three men left, they are allowed to move to any free spot, without moving along the lines. This makes it easier for them to stop the other player making mills. When one player has only two men left, they have lost the game.

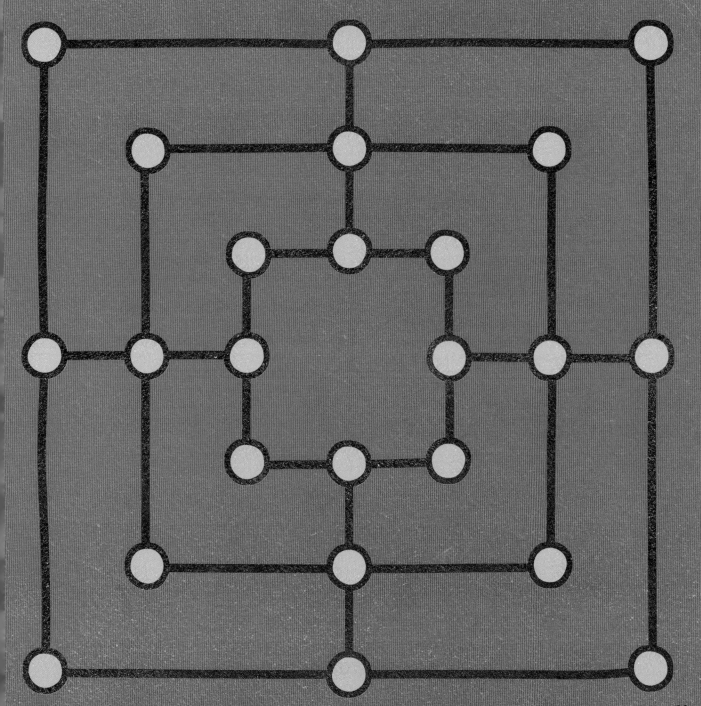

51

GREAT MINDS...

...think alike, so they say. Find out if it's true
with these games.

TOO SWEET

Two players put a coat or blanket
between them and hide some
differently colored or flavored candies
under it. Each then reaches for a candy
and pulls it out.

If the candies are the same, both
players can keep or eat them. If they
are different, they have to put them
back.

The game continues until all the
candies have been won or both players
feel they have had enough – of the
candies or the game!

MONEY MATCH

A similar game can be played with coins.
This time, a selection of small coins is
placed under the blanket. Both players
feel for a coin and pull it out.

Someone who can't see the game then
shouts "Higher!" or "Lower!" If they yell
"Higher!" the player with the higher coin
wins and keeps both coins. If "Lower!" is
called, the person with the lower coin is
the winner and keeps both coins. If both
coins are the same, they are put back and
the players try again.

The game goes on until all the coins have
been won.

TOUCH TALK

Our fingertips have oodles of nerve endings, so they are very sensitive, but that's not true of everywhere on our bodies. Try these ticklish tests to see for yourself.

Ask your partner to shut their eyes. No peeking!

1. Taking your partner's hand, "write" a letter or a number on their palm with your fingertip. Can they tell what it was? Try a short word next.

2. Now try writing on the back of their hand or on their wrist. Where can they feel most accurately?

3. Try the experiment the other way around. Is it the same for you?

If your friend agrees, you can try writing on other parts of the body, such as knees, back, or even feet. Just make sure the "reader" can't see what is being written. Then it's a true touch test.

ODDS OR EVENS

You don't need any counters or boards for this game.
Just a partner to play with and your two hands.

One of you chooses ODDS and the other EVENS.

Both of you form your hands into fists and, waving them up and down,
say, "One, two, three!" Immediately after shouting "three!" you both hold
up your hands showing however many fingers you want, with
the rest tucked into your palms.

Count all the fingers that both of you are showing. If it is an odd number,
the person who chose ODDS gets a point. If EVENS,
then that person wins the point.

Carry on playing until one of you has ten points
and is declared the winner.

GOAL!

This is not a page. This is the back
of a soccer goal!

Read the instructions below, then
fold down the page along the dotted
line and turn to page 57.

1. Have a penalty shoot-out with some
of your travel buddies. First make a ball
by scrunching up some candy wrappers
or scrap paper.

2. Place the ball on the spot on the field
marked on page 57 and flick it towards
the goal. Your opponent is allowed to
defend the goal with one downward-
pointing finger.

3. Take turns taking five penalties each.
If you both have the same
score, keep shooting until you have
a clear winner.

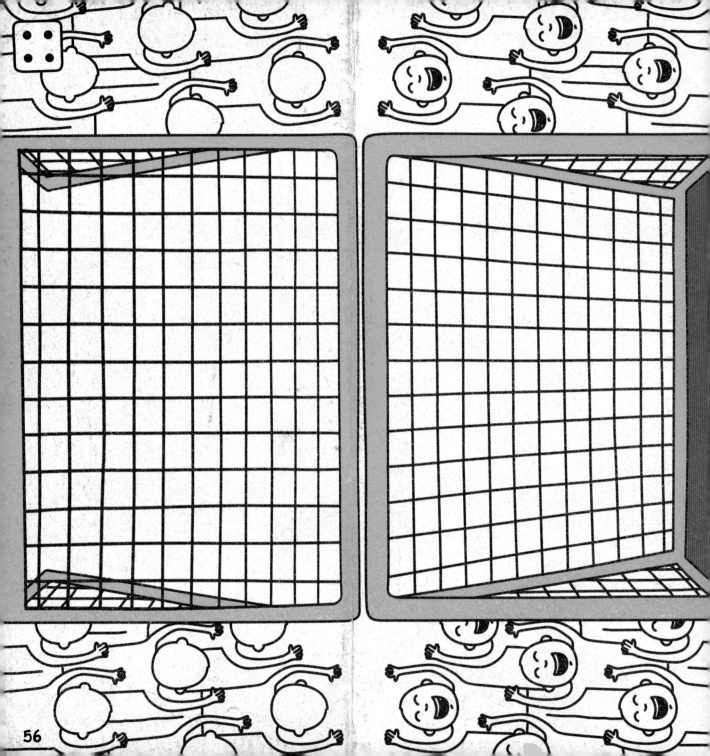

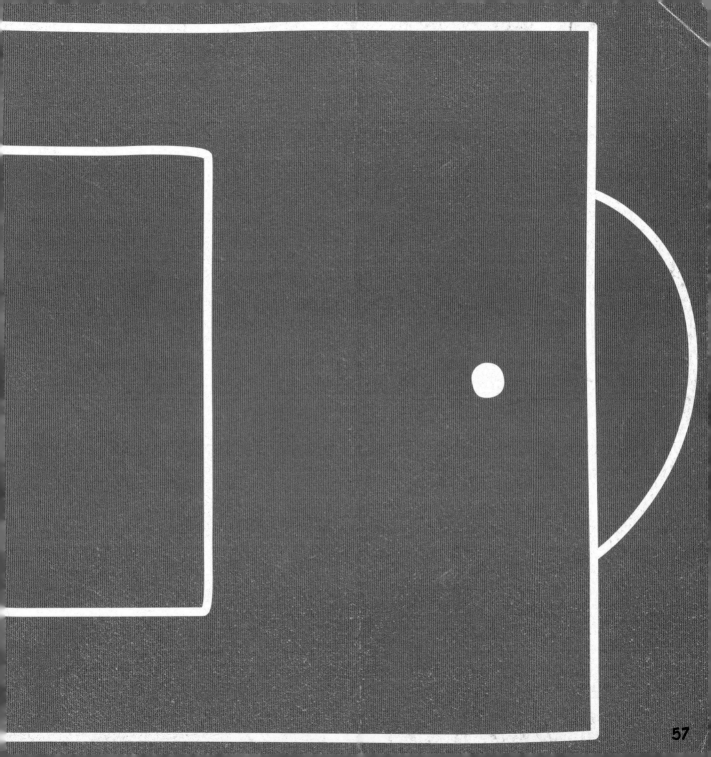

CHAMPION SIGHTSEEING

This game is similar to others you may have played but involves increasing numbers of objects and there's no alphabetical order to give you a clue. Play with as many travel buddies as you can. Any player who makes a mistake is out.

The first player says, "On my journey I saw one tree."

The next might say, "On my journey I saw one tree and two churches."

The third could add, "On my journey I saw one tree, two churches, and three trucks," and so on.

Try playing it first with things you might really see. Players can challenge if they don't think it's likely. Then try with wilder ideas. "On my journey I saw one elephant, two marathon runners, three chocolate sundaes, four alien spacecraft...."

Which is easier to remember?

STAR CAR

Give yourself a time limit for this game and agree on some house rules – well, car rules.

Each person chooses a different color and counts the number of cars they see in that color in the time allowed – say, half an hour. The winner is the player to count the highest number of cars.

Your own game rules might include:
- only counting cars coming towards you.
- only counting cars that are moving.
- only counting cars that are not moving.
- only counting cars that are just one color.
- allowing cars that are at least half the color.

Car colors, believe it or not, have fashion trends. If, for example, silver cars have recently been all the rage, you might decide to leave those out of your game, as one person would have a massive advantage.

Some families play by choosing colors randomly (order of age of players and order of the next few cars that come past).

There are some variations you can play, as well.

ALIEN CAR

Players choose unusual colors – orange, purple, pink, or yellow – and these become "alien cars." The person to spot the smallest number is the winner. It's fun, too, to pretend to fear the alien cars and duck down in your seats when they pass.

FRONT AND BACK

Those in the front seats can only count cars coming towards them (but have a better view), while those in the back seats can count any cars (but may have the backs of large heads blocking their sightlines).

HOW MANY WIGGLY WORMS?

These little critters are not easy to count. Can you guesstimate how many there are? Challenge a travel buddy and see which of you is closest to the answer on page 127.

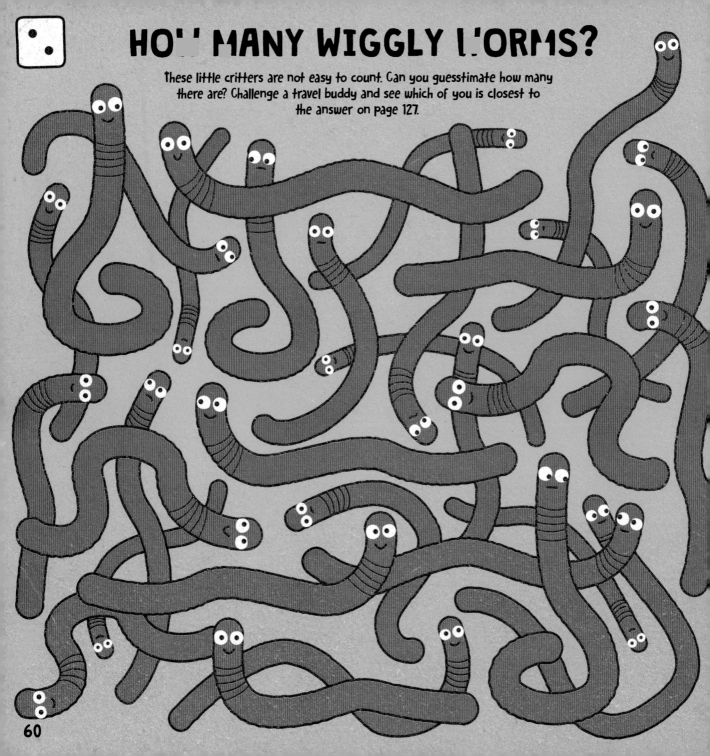

ODD ONE OUT

Here's a word search with a difference. Look at the list of capital cities below. Which one CAN'T you find in the word search? Turn to page 127 to find out if you're right.

T	T	N	E	K	H	S	A	T	E	A	D
R	Q	A	U	I	E	P	I	A	T	N	R
K	A	V	G	L	L	A	L	I	N	A	M
E	W	U	A	O	S	I	R	A	P	J	R
O	A	S	R	N	I	S	A	M	I	L	E
H	T	A	P	D	N	A	I	R	O	B	I
D	T	N	L	O	K	I	V	S	V	U	Z
N	O	T	G	N	I	L	L	E	W	J	A
I	T	I	A	I	F	O	S	B	C	L	G
W	I	A	A	T	O	G	O	B	U	L	R
N	U	G	O	I	M	A	D	R	I	D	E
T	Q	O	K	A	M	A	B	Z	H	J	B

BAMAKO
BOGOTA
DUBLIN
HELSINKI
LIMA
LONDON
LJUBLJANA
MADRID
MANILA
NAIROBI
OSLO
OTTAWA
PARIS
PRAGUE
QUITO
SANTIAGO
SEOUL
SOFIA
SUVA
TAIPEI
TASHKENT
WELLINGTON
WINDHOEK
ZAGREB

Play this with a friend and fill one board each. Decide if the winner is going to be the first to finish their board or the first to complete a row or a column. Cover the squares with coins or candies or candy wrappers as you spot the items shown on your board.

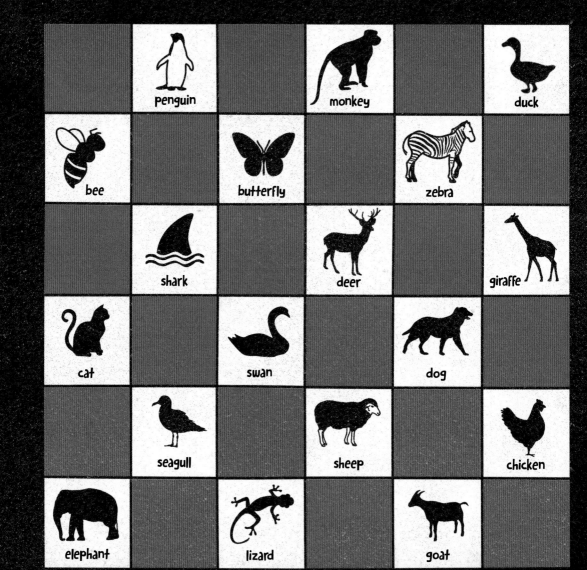

You don't have to see a real animal to cover a square. It might be a picture of an animal on a road sign or truck, the name of a restaurant, town, or street, or a T-shirt or cuddly toy.

	elephant		gorilla		swan
cat		goat		parrot	
	monkey		seagull		camel
snake		mouse		horse	
	dog		octopus		chicken
sheep		giraffe		frog	

TARGET WORD

You will need small coins or candies in two different colors. Decide which color means "yes" and which means "no."

This is a game for two players. One player thinks of a category, such as animals, cars, or cities. The other player thinks of a word in that category. It is up to the first player to guess it by naming a letter in the word. If the letter appears in the word, put a "yes" candy or coin on it. If not, put a "no" candy or coin.

Play continues until the word is guessed. The number of coins or candies on the page at that point is the guesser's score. Then the other player has a turn. The winner, when you decide to stop, is the player with the lowest score. Players are allowed to peek under "yes" coins or candies to remind themselves of the letters already known.

D   P

R   K   M   E

Z   X   I

B

J   T   H   S   V

A

W   L   Y

F   Q

O   G   U   C   N

FUTURE FANTASY

Follow the timeline with your finger – there are some twists and turns ahead! When you come to a stopwatch, stop! Imagine yourself a year from now. Where will you be? What will you be doing? Then go on. At each stopwatch, imagine another year into the future. Make your imaginings amazing. You have to have wishes to have wishes come true!

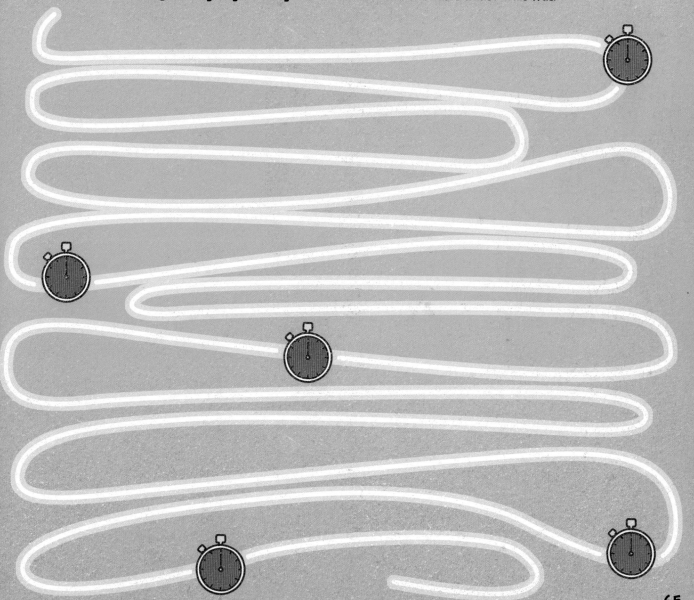

REMEMBER, REMEMBER

If you practiced with the memory game on page 7, it's time to try something trickier. This game has twice as many objects but you are allowed two minutes to look at them. Then turn the page and see how many of the 20 you can remember.

Play by yourself or challenge a friend. See if it helps to tell yourself a crazy story involving all the items pictured here.

LINE UP! (READ THIS FIRST)

You happened to be in the jewelry store when a robber walked in and stole an expensive diamond ring. The police have mug shots of a whole list of suspects. Can your travel buddy play police officer and find out who you saw? Instructions for you are on page 69, and instructions for your travel buddy are on page 71. Good luck!

HOW TO BE A GOOD CITIZEN...

First lift up this page so that your travel buddy can't see the mug shots below.

Then place a candy or coin on the dastardly devil you saw robbing the jewelry store. (You can choose anyone you want.)

Now tell your buddy that they have to ask you questions to find out who the criminal is. They have some suggestions about what to ask on the next page and all the same pictures in front of them as you have.

Make sure you answer carefully and truthfully (unless it was you that did it, of course).

69

INTERVIEW TECHNIQUES

Ask whichever of these questions might be helpful, or make up some of your own:

Were they wearing a hat?

Were they wearing glasses?

Did they have a beard?

Did they have blue or pink hair?

LINE UP! (READ THIS FIRST)

There has been a theft at the local jewelry store. Luckily, you have an eyewitness sitting across from you but they are hesitating to point out the thief. You will need to ask some probing questions to get to the truth of the matter. Arm yourself with some coins or candies to put on the mug shots below as you eliminate them from your inquiries. In the end, the one with no coin or candy should be the villain! On the interview room wall in front of you are some reminders of the kinds of things you might like to ask. You don't have to stick to these questions though.
The best police officers aren't afraid to get creative. Good luck!

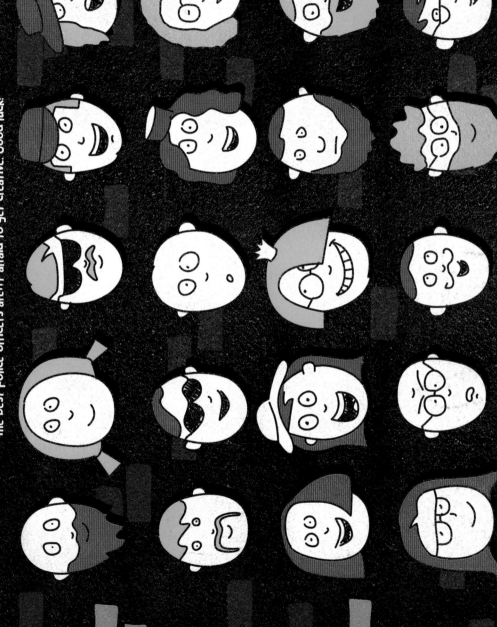

BRIDGES

A word game for two people or two teams, this can be over in seconds or go on for hours. Get ready to tell a seriously sly story!

One person shuts their eyes and points somewhere on the list of starting phrases. Someone from the other team does the same for the right-hand list to give a finishing phrase. One person from each team takes turns saying three or four words. The aim of the game for the starting team is to make a "word bridge" to get to the finish and for the finishing team it's to stop them.

For example, if the starting phrase was "The curious cat..." and the finishing phrase was "into the haunted house," the game might go like this:

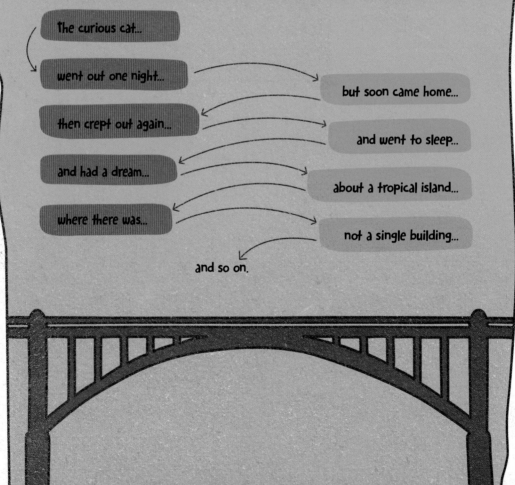

The curious cat...

went out one night...

but soon came home...

then crept out again...

and went to sleep...

and had a dream...

about a tropical island...

where there was...

not a single building...

and so on.

The mountain's summit...

Behind the ancient wall...

Long ago in Africa...

There was once a red lizard...

One stormy night...

...straight into the hot saucepan.

...covered in blue feathers.

...a brand-new planet.

...beside the walrus.

...inside her ear.

TIME TEST

We all have an inner clock. It's time to test yours and your travel buddies', too.

Someone with a watch with a second hand or a phone with a stopwatch on it will be the timer.

The timer says, "Start!" and everyone else (definitely without looking at their own watches or phones) shouts "Now!" when they think that exactly one minute has passed.

The timer waits until everyone has shouted, then lets them know who was the closest to one minute. You could try a few times to see if you improve.

You could try:

– counting slowly to 60 seconds by saying "one elephant, two elephants..."

– counting your breaths as you breathe calmly in and out.

CHATTERBOX

Sometimes you don't want to play a game. You just want to chat to your fellow travelers and find out a bit more about them. Even people you think you know really well can surprise you.

Try asking some of these questions. You may get some interesting answers!

Who would you like to play you in a film about your life? Why?

If you could have any pet, which would you choose?

What is your earliest memory?

If you won millions in the lottery, what would you do?

If you could travel back in time, when and where would you choose?

What three things would you like to achieve in the next year?

What would you like to be really, really good at?

WHO DID I CHOOSE?

Here's one of those infuriating games that is so obvious once you
know the secret but perplexingly puzzling until then.
You need a few people to play. Here's how.

One person slowly points their finger at each person in the group, in a
random order, then asks, "Who did I choose?"

Someone might say, "Was it Harry?" and the chooser says, "No!" Eventually,
someone will ask, "Was it me?" and the answer is "Yes!"

The game is repeated until someone guesses how the choice is made. It's not
anything to do with the pointing. It's the person who speaks first!

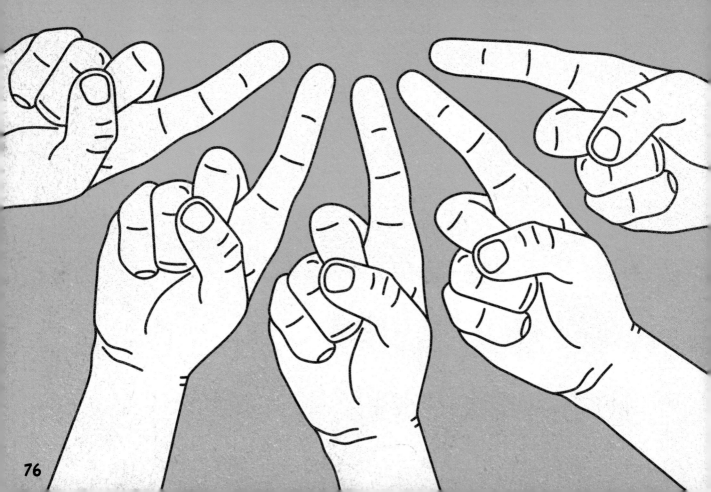

HOW MANY SQUARES?

How many squares can you find in the picture below? Don't forget, some squares together might make another square. Turn to page 127 to check your answer.

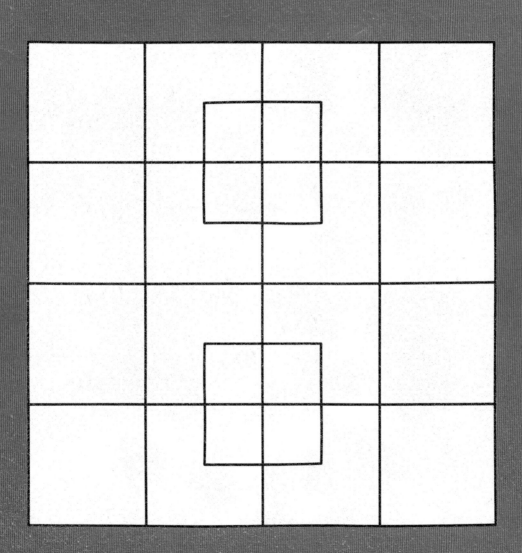

TOWN TRAIL

Test your map skills by turning the book and sharing it with your travel buddy.
Lift page 79, so that you can see the instructions as well as your map below.
Your friend also has a copy of the map and another set of instructions
on pages 80 and 81.

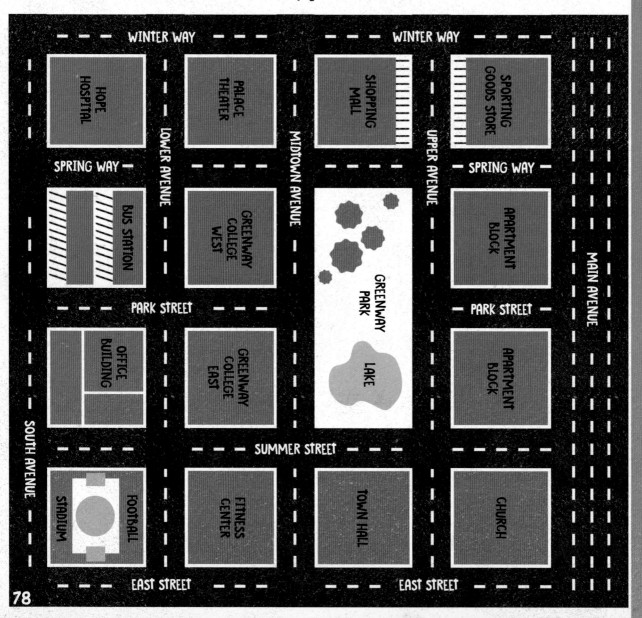

WINTER WAY

WINTER WAY

HOPE HOSPITAL

PALACE THEATER

SHOPPING MALL

SPORTING GOODS STORE

LOWER AVENUE

MIDTOWN AVENUE

UPPER AVENUE

SPRING WAY

SPRING WAY

BUS STATION

GREENWAY COLLEGE WEST

GREENWAY PARK

APARTMENT BLOCK

MAIN AVENUE

PARK STREET

PARK STREET

OFFICE BUILDING

GREENWAY COLLEGE EAST

LAKE

APARTMENT BLOCK

GREENWAY RIVER

SUMMER STREET

SOUTH AVENUE

FOOTBALL STADIUM

FITNESS CENTER

TOWN HALL

CHURCH

EAST STREET

EAST STREET

Read aloud each of the below sets of instructions for your partner to follow on their own map. Then see how well you follow their directions.

FEELING FIT!

1. Out for a morning run, you set out from your apartment on the corner of Summer Street and Upper Avenue and run counterclockwise all the way around the park.

2. Back on Summer Street, you jog down towards the football stadium and turn right onto Lower Avenue.

3. After two blocks, you feel exhausted. What cunning plan do you have to get home quickly and easily?

SHOE SHOPPING

1. After a picnic lunch with your pals in the park, you decide to buy some new sneakers and head to the mall.

2. You can't find the color you want anywhere, so you cross Upper Avenue in the hope that the sporting goods store might have what you need.

3. It's hopeless again, but they suggest the store at the fitness center. Which way will you go to get there?

4. Success! You celebrate by jogging home up Summer Street.

WEDDING DAY

1. Your aunt is getting married today in the church. It's really near your home. But before the ceremony, you have to go to the bus station to meet your cousin. You want to pick up some theater tickets on the way. Which way will you go?

2. Your cousin is wearing three-inch heels! You catch a taxi outside Hope Hospital, but the driver is new in town. He needs directions to the church. There's a football game on, so you direct him the long way around, avoiding the stadium. What do you tell him?

DAD DELIVERY

1. You're at Greenway College West when your dad calls you from his office on Lower Avenue. He wants you to pick up his dry cleaning from the mall. You dash off to do it quickly. Which way do you go?

2. When you deliver to your dad, he rewards you by taking you to lunch at the fitness center café, before leaving you to return to his office. Which street will you take to get home?

79

When you've had some practice following directions, read each of the sets of instructions below for your partner to follow on their own map. Then make up some more of your own.

WHERE'S FIFI?

1. Your friend Amy, who lives on the corner of Upper Avenue and Spring Way, has lost her cat, Fifi. You make some posters to put up all around town, including the mall, the sporting goods store, the theater, the bus station, and the fitness center. Figure out a route for delivering the posters.

2. All your hard work has paid off! Fifi was found sitting in the sun next to the lake. How many blocks was she from home?

FAN-TASTIC!

1. Amazing! Your favorite singer is coming to perform at the Palace Theater. The only trouble is that the line for tickets stretches right down Lower Avenue. There's so much demand that the organizers decide to put the show on at the football stadium instead. How many blocks is that from the theater?

2. The show is awesome – and loud! The music can be heard inside the church. How many blocks away is that?

OUCH!

1. Setting off from Greenway College West, you join a protest march about the need to make a safe playground in Greenway Park. A petition is handed in to the Town Hall. Which street is it on?

2. Ooops! You slip on the Town Hall steps and hurt your ankle. Your friend helps you to walk to Hope Hospital. Which is the quietest, quickest route to get there?

3. How many blocks is it from the hospital to your apartment on Spring Way?

SIGHTSEEING

1. If you stand by the lake in Greenway Park, you have a good view of the five nearest buildings. What are they?

2. If you were creating a Town Trail for tourists, what route would it take and which sights would it include along the way? Try it out on your travel buddy in your best tour Leader tones.

TOWN TRAIL

Use this map to test a friend's map-reading skills and your own! You'll soon know this town better than your hometown!

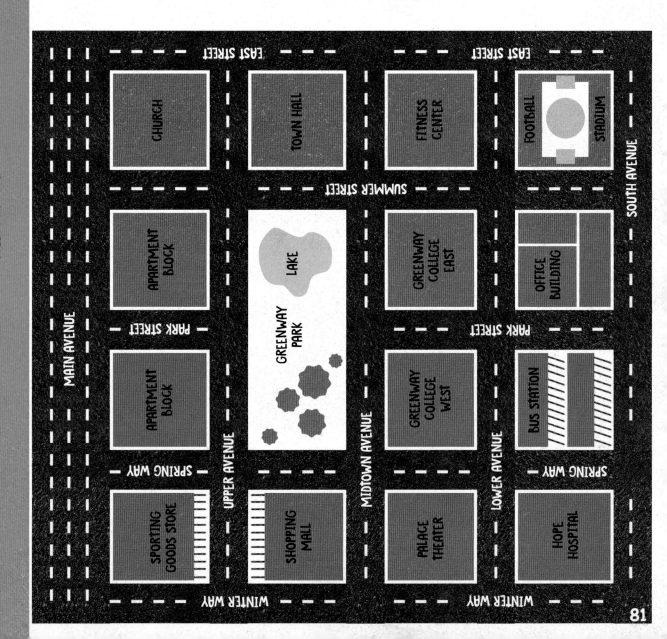

WATERY WORD SEARCH

More of the surface of Earth is water than ... well .... earth. Find these oceans, seas, rivers, and lakes in the word search below, but which one in the list ISN'T in the grid? Turn to page 127 to check your answer.

E	B	A	I	K	A	L	I	Y	Q	K	F	E	Z	M
R	T	G	A	N	G	E	S	T	G	J	H	S	I	N
I	C	H	A	N	G	J	I	A	N	G	U	S	A	I
E	B	A	R	E	N	T	S	J	N	D	S	E	S	P
L	L	I	U	M	I	U	A	R	N	I	N	Z	U	Z
I	S	O	O	C	Y	M	E	I	S	A	A	U	P	B
N	L	A	A	A	A	H	V	S	R	L	K	D	E	A
A	N	C	D	Z	T	I	I	R	C	N	I	A	R	L
E	A	E	O	U	C	P	E	L	I	A	Y	N	I	T
B	R	N	O	T	P	T	E	A	T	I	N	U	O	I
B	E	S	O	I	I	R	D	R	N	P	A	B	R	C
I	N	R	V	D	D	K	M	C	A	S	G	E	M	Z
R	I	B	E	X	P	A	Z	T	L	A	N	E	D	F
A	E	M	V	N	I	Z	W	I	T	C	A	N	N	O
C	S	N	A	I	D	N	I	C	A	D	T	L	H	N

SEAS
BALTIC
BARENTS
CARIBBEAN
CASPIAN
MEDITERRANEAN
RED

OCEANS
ARCTIC
ATLANTIC
INDIAN
PACIFIC
SOUTHERN

RIVERS
AMAZON
CHANG JIANG
DANUBE
GANGES
INDUS
MISSISSIPPI
NILE
SEINE

LAKES
BAIKAL
ERIE
SUPERIOR
TANGANYIKA
TITICACA
VICTORIA

ADVENTURES AHOY!

You're sure to have adventures on your travels. Get ready now with some dream discoveries. Imagine you are the captain of a ship, sailing the seven seas. Follow a route between the islands slowly with your finger. When you feel like it, stop off at an island. What do you see, hear, and feel there? What adventures do you have? When you are ready, sail on to your next discovery.

LAUGHING NOT ALLOWED!

Sometimes nothing is funnier than seeing someone trying
not to smile, smirk, giggle, or gurgle.

Choose one of your travel buddies and ask everyone with you to do
whatever they can to make them smile or laugh. Touching is not allowed, so
tickling is out, but you could try:

making a silly face

telling your best joke

winking each eye one at a time

wiggling your ears (if you can!)

looking very, very serious

looking them right in the eye and not blinking

wiggling your finger weirdly

making animal noises

making your hair look mad

doing your best dance moves sitting down

looking away, then suddenly back again

putting on a funny voice

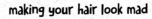

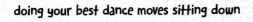

Your pal, of course, has to look deadly serious. Time how long it takes
them to give up. Let everyone have a turn. Who's the the most scarily
serious in your group?

MAZE RACE

Race your travel pal to the treasure at the center of the maze. One of you starts with a finger on A, the other on B. Three, two, one, GO! Each of you must carefully follow the maze with a finger to reach the center first. Don't even think about cheating – you might end up back where you started!

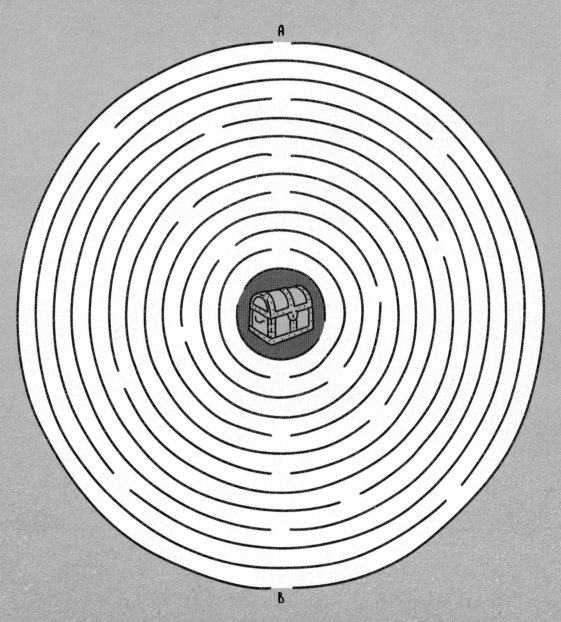

ALPHABET LISTS

There's no pencil or paper needed for our version of this famous game.

First, choose a category by asking the youngest player to close their eyes and put a finger anywhere on these two pages. The category nearest to their finger is what you use.

Then one person announces the first letter: "A!" Everyone yells out a word that begins with A and fits the category. So if the category was Colors, for example, you might hear: "Apricot!" "Aubergine!" "Apple green!" "Avocado!" "Amber!" (That's quite a hard one!)

You need to be quick. If someone shouts your word before you do, you get one more try after everyone has shouted. Then you move on to the next letter. Anyone who can't think of a word that fits loses a life. Starting with ten lives is easiest, because you can count them down on your fingers!

The winner is the person with most lives left at the end of the alphabet, or the last man standing if everyone else loses lives really quickly!

CLOTHES

SOMETHING YOU CAN LIVE IN

THINGS FOUND IN A KITCHEN

CARS

SONG TITLES

FOOD

MOVIES

BOOKS

DOGS

FLOWERS

A B C D E F G H I J K L M

BIRDS COLORS COUNTRIES

TV CHARACTERS TREES TOYS

PARTS OF THE BODY BOYS' NAMES

ANIMALS CITIES SPORTS

JOBS PEOPLE DO DRINKS BANDS

FRUIT AND VEG UNDERWATER CREATURES

THINGS IN THE SKY ICE-CREAM FLAVORS

GIRLS' NAMES MUSICAL INSTRUMENTS

N O P Q R S T U V W X Y Z

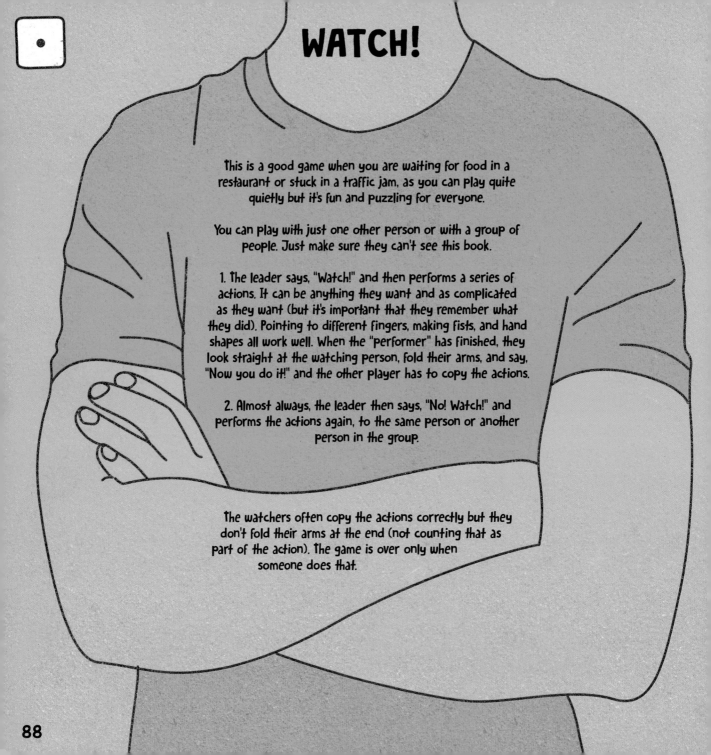

WATCH!

This is a good game when you are waiting for food in a restaurant or stuck in a traffic jam, as you can play quite quietly but it's fun and puzzling for everyone.

You can play with just one other person or with a group of people. Just make sure they can't see this book.

1. The leader says, "Watch!" and then performs a series of actions. It can be anything they want and as complicated as they want (but it's important that they remember what they did). Pointing to different fingers, making fists, and hand shapes all work well. When the "performer" has finished, they look straight at the watching person, fold their arms, and say, "Now you do it!" and the other player has to copy the actions.

2. Almost always, the leader then says, "No! Watch!" and performs the actions again, to the same person or another person in the group.

The watchers often copy the actions correctly but they don't fold their arms at the end (not counting that as part of the action). The game is over only when someone does that.

WHAT'S BEEN LOST?

Here's a weird collection of odd items that passengers have left on a train.
Take a long look at the picture, then turn to page 90.
You can do this by yourself or play with a friend. If two of you are playing,
make sure you can both see the picture clearly for the same amount of time.

WHAT'S BEEN FOUND?

Here's that strange selection of lost property again. But someone has come and claimed one item. Without looking back, can you spot which it was? Only look back at page 89 if you get really stuck. If you're still stumped, turn to page 127 for the answer.

HEADS AND TAILS

This is a good game for lots of people to play, or for a few people when you need to choose someone to go first or to go and get the ice cream.

You need any two coins and someone to toss them.

The coin-tosser says, "Heads or tails?"

Each player guesses how the coins are going to fall when they are tossed.

If they think there will be two heads, they put both hands on their head.

If they think there will be two tails, they put both hands on their rear end.

If they think one head and one tail, no prizes for guessing it's one hand on their head and one on their rear end.

The coin-tosser tosses and announces the result. Anyone who got it wrong is out. Anyone who got it right is still in the game and plays again until only one person is left.

TIC-TAC-TOE

Play this game with a friend, using counters instead of pen and paper.
You'll each need five counters of two different colors or shapes.
Coins or candies would be fine.

Take turns placing one counter on the grid. The winner is the first
to complete a row of three of their counters, up, across, or diagonally.

If you are evenly matched, the game often ends in a draw,
but some players are hard to beat...

FROM THREE TO FOUR

If you are good at tic-tac-toe, you'll have a head start with this game. The rules are the same — take turns placing a counter on the grid — but this time you need to make a row (across, up and down, or diagonally) of FOUR counters to win. (You'll each need more counters.)

The other difference is that you need to think of the grid as a jar. Counters can't float in midair. Rows need to be built from the bottom of the grid.

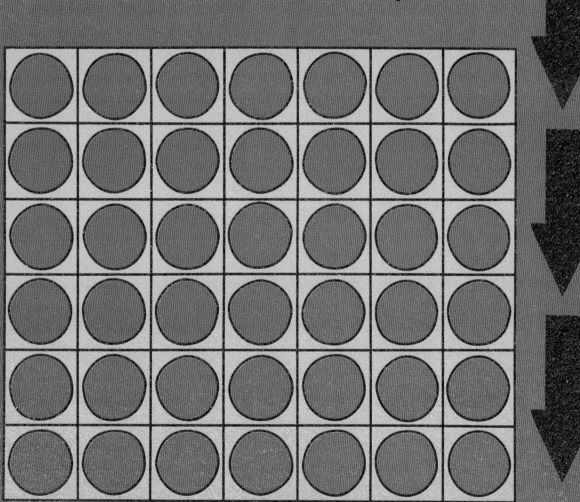

HUNGER GAME

There's nothing dangerous about this, but it may make you hungry!
Any number can play. If it's too easy, try the variations below.

The first player says, "I was hungry when I packed my bag, so in it I put an apple" (or another food item beginning with A).

The next player says, "I was hungry when I packed my bag, so in it I put an apple and a brownie."

And so on. Each player must remember the list of foods mentioned so far as well as adding a new one. Anyone who forgets is out.

If you get to the end of the alphabet, just keep going from A again, remembering all of the first list as well.

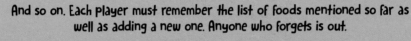

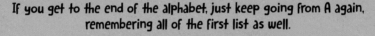

THIRSTY WORK

"I was thirsty when I packed my bag, so in it I put some apple juice..." Adults in the car will decide which kinds of drinks you are allowed just for this game!

MONOGRAM MEAL

This time, stick with just one letter and keep going until one person can't think of anything else to eat that begins with the chosen letter. You may have to be inventive. "I was hungry when I packed my bag, so in it I put a bagel, a boiled potato, a burned sausage, a broken egg..."

DON'T SAY IT!

It sounds easy, but how good are you at watching what you say?

No matter what question you are asked, you mustn't say "yes" or "no."
You can say anything else but not those words. It is the other players' job to trip you up
so that you say the forbidden words and they can take your place.
So if you are asked if you are 87 years old, for example (and you're not!), you could say:

"Not exactly..."

"I wouldn't say that."

"Do I look like I'm 87 years old?"

"Absolutely not!"

"I would have to answer in the negative."

"That would be a wrong assumption."

"You must be joking!"

...and so on, but you mustn't shout "NO!"

THAT WOULD BE AN AFFIRMATIVE.

I GUESS SO.

YOU ARE CORRECT.

THAT WOULD BE A NEGATIVE.

I DON'T THINK SO.

YOU ARE INCORRECT.

OR THIS!

You can change the game to make other
words the ones to be avoided. Some
difficult ones are:

I, you, the, a, errr...

LUDO

It's probably best not to play this if hurtling down a bumpy road. Your counters will bounce! But it's great for boring stretches of highway or long flights.

You need four counters for each player, in different colors or shapes so you know whose counter is whose. Different coins or colored candies work well.

You also need a dice. If you don't have one or a dice app on a phone, flick the first 94 pages of this book and stop randomly on any left-hand page for the score in the top left corner.

1. Place your counters on one of the large outer squares. That is now your "color."

2. Take turns throwing (or flicking) the dice. The highest score starts, with players following in clockwise order.

3. You need to throw a six to start moving a counter out of your starting area and around the board on the white squares in a clockwise direction. When you get a six, you can also have another turn.

4. If you land on another player's counter, that counter goes back to the starting area. They have to get a six to start it moving again.

5. Your aim is to get all your counters home to the middle. When you are nearly home, you go up the colored path to your home space. Once you have a counter on your colored path, it is safe. You need to throw the exact number to get it to home.

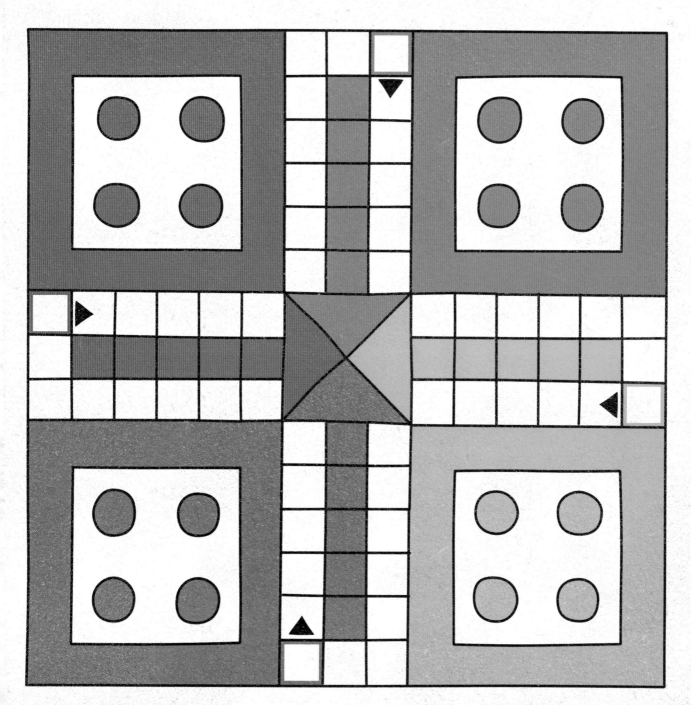

ACTING UP

If you have drama queens and kings in your party, test their
theatrical talents on our stage page.

MIME TIME

Choose an activity to mime and see if
everyone can guess what you
are doing. Remember, no words or
sounds of any kind are allowed.
Start with simple actions, like brushing
your hair, and move on to trickier
tasks, such as making a sandwich or
going to the dentist.

Another hilarious mime challenge is
to act like an animal. Ask an adult to
whisper a suggestion and then try to
act so that your pals guess it. It's not
so easy with no sounds allowed, and
your alligator impression may leave
them giggling too hard to guess.

FEELING FINE

Choose an ordinary action, such as
reading a book or brushing your teeth.
Then act out the action with a
particular emotion in mind.
For example, you could do it:

angrily	bravely
lazily	proudly
sadly	lovingly
excitedly	thoughtfully
terrified	guiltily
shyly	grumpily
hesitantly	happily

The person who correctly guesses what
you're doing, or comes closest to
guessing, has the next turn.

FINGER GYM

Try these handy exercises. The second one may surprise you.

1. Put your hand flat on the page. Keeping the other fingers flat on the page, lift each finger in turn. Repeat this, a little faster each time. Which fingers are speediest?

2. Keeping the other fingers flat, try to bend each finger in turn so that your nail is flat on the page (as if you were making a fist but with one finger at a time). Can you do it with ALL your fingers, always keeping the others flat?

TRANSPORT BINGO

Play this with a friend and take one board each. Decide if the winner is going to be the first to finish their board or the first to complete a row or a column. Cover the squares on your board with coins, candies, or candy wrappers when you spot each item.

mail truck		vintage car		tow truck	
	supermarket trolley		digger		refrigerated truck
taxi		bicycle		concrete mixer	
	motor scooter		minibus		hearse
fire engine		rickshaw		sailboat	
	bus		train		motorbike

It doesn't matter where you see these vehicles. They could be on the road, in a magazine, or in a showroom. (This book doesn't count!)

taxi		beverage truck		sailboat	
police car		train		ice-cream van
ambulance		motorbike		tanker truck	
	digger		hot-air balloon		vintage car
minibus		rowboat		garbage truck	
	motor coach		suitcase on wheels		motor scooter

MEMORY MADNESS

You've had a lot of practice now, so here are a crazy number of objects. Yes, there are 40 of them, but don't worry. You don't have to be able to list them all, but you do have to notice them.

Give yourself three minutes. Then pass the book to a friend. Your buddy makes sure you can't see and asks you ten questions. For example, "Is there a penguin?" You have to answer "Yes!" or "No!" It's up to your questioner to name ten objects – some will be there and some won't. How well will you score?

If you are too, too good at this, your friend can ask more cunning questions. "Is there anything that can fly?" "Is there anything with two feet?" "Is there anything that you have in your bedroom at home?"

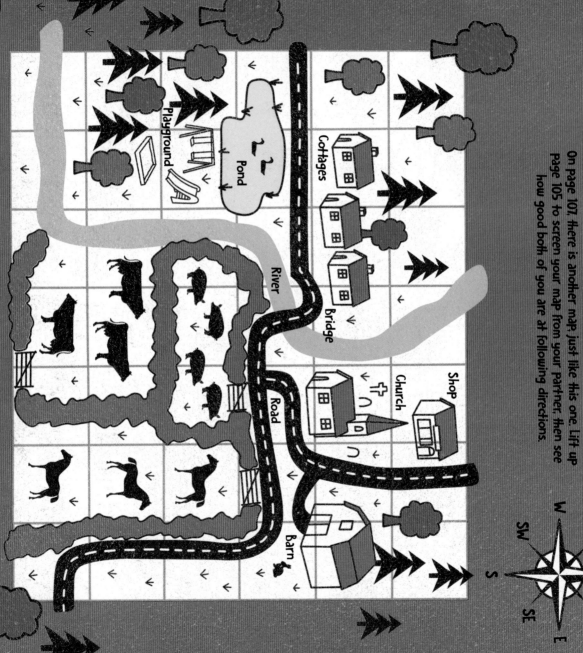

MAP MAZE

On Page 107, there is another map, just like this one. Lift up Page 105 to screen your map from your partner, then see how good both of you are at following directions.

Pond

Playground

Cottages

River

Bridge

Road

Church

Shop

Barn

BEHIND YOU!

1. You are walking along a road in a northerly direction, with a hedge on your left.

2. The road bends to the left and you come to a gate. You turn to lean over it. What can you see?

3. What is behind you?

HAND-HOLDING

1. You are in the shop with your little brother, buying him an ice cream.

2. He wants to go to the playground. Do you turn left or right when you leave the shop?

3. Do you need to head southwest or northeast to reach the playground?

4. As soon as he gets to the playground, your little brother spots some cows. He wants to run straight into their field. Why can't he?

HEEL, HENRY!

1. You are taking your dog for a walk beside the river, heading south. He loves to get wet, so you have to keep him on the leash. As well as the river, there's another tempting splashing point. What is it?

2. You carry on beside the river as it turns westward. Instead of going back the way you came, you decide to take a shortcut towards the road. What do you see all around you as you head north?

ESCAPE!

1. You've been helping to cut the grass in the churchyard. As you leave, something small and pink dashes past you.

2. You turn right out of the church gate. When you reach the t-junction, you see someone has left a gate open in front of you. What is usually in that field?

105

When you have had some practice following directions, read each of the sets of instructions below for your partner to follow on their own map. Then make up some more of your own.

ESCAPE!

1. You have borrowed a friend's rowboat and are floating along the river when you hear someone walking above your head. Where are you exactly?

2. If the next thing you see is a little pond, are you traveling north or south along the river?

PHOTO FINISH

A friend's birthday party features a photo treasure hunt, where players have to bring back photos of the places on a list. Here is the list:

horse   pine tree   gate

duck   gate

gravestone   chimney   seesaw

What is the quickest route around the village to be able to return with all the photos to the garden of the most easterly cottage, where the party is taking place?

SHOPPING

1. Your friend lives in the middle cottage of a row of three. When you visit, she is unwell and asks you to walk to the shop to get her some juice. Do you have to cross the road to get there?

2. Do you have to cross anything else?

3. Do you have to cross the road on the way back to your friend's cottage?

GOING AHEAD

1. You meet your friend on the bridge over the river. He has a quick errand to run and asks you to go on ahead. He gives you directions to a large building in the east of the village. Does he ask you to walk east or west? What other directions does he give you?

2. When you reach the large building, you see a creature nibbling the grass. What is it?

MAP MAZE

Turn to page 104 to see how to use this map to test a friend's map-reading and your own! Are you a master of map-reading?

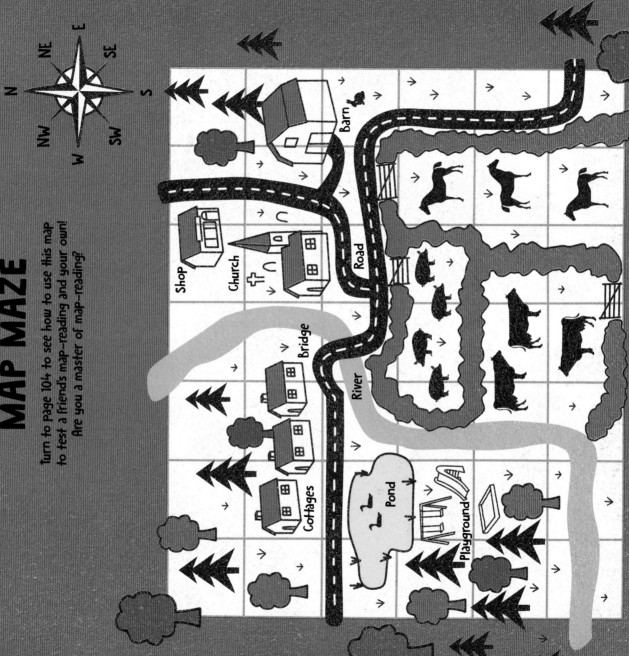

HAZARDS AND DETOURS

Straight roads with no roadwork, floods, or traffic jams are a driver's dream. Unfortunately, this journey is more of a nightmare. Can you reach your destination at the top of the mountain without disaster?

Each player has a counter, which can be a piece of candy or a coin. You also need a dice. If you don't have one lying around, or a dice app on your phone, simply flick through the first 100 pages of this book (being careful not to disturb page 109) and stop randomly. Then use the number that appears on the dice at the top left of the page.

1. All players place their counters on the start and take turns throwing the dice (or flicking the pages on your left). They need a six to start, and throwing a six at any time in the game also allows them an extra throw.

2. Players move along the road as many spaces as the dice shows. If they land on a hazard, the road has been closed. The vehicle (counter) slides back down, just like in a game of Chutes and Ladders.

If players land on a detour, they can bypass dangerous conditions ahead and zoom off to reach their destination faster.

3. The winner is the first to reach the finish.

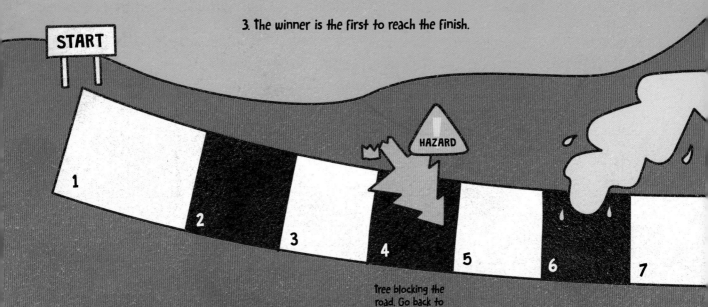

START

HAZARD

1 2 3 4 5 6 7

Tree blocking the road. Go back to the start while the road is cleared.

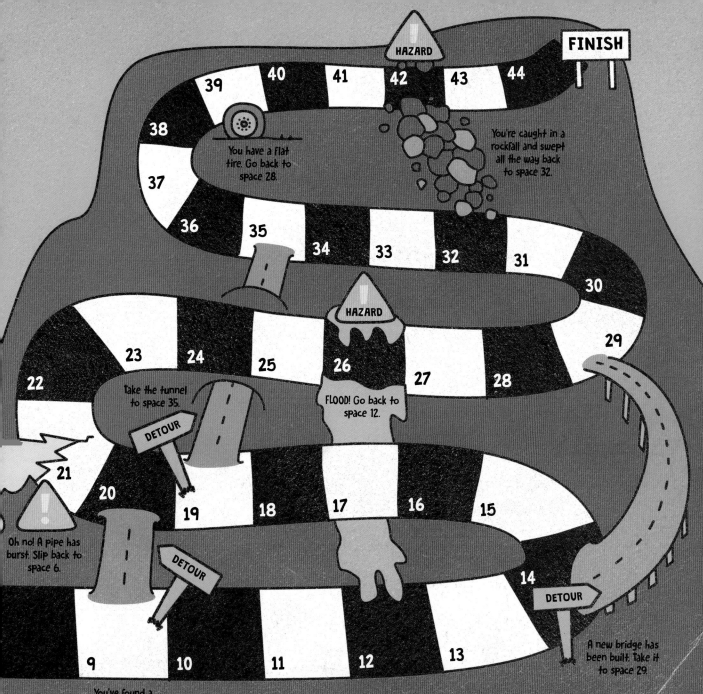

HAZARD

FINISH

39 40 41 42 43 44

38

37

You have a flat tire. Go back to space 28.

You're caught in a rockfall and swept all the way back to space 32.

36 35 34 33 32 31

30

HAZARD

23 24 25 26 27 28

29

22

Take the tunnel to space 35.

DETOUR

FLOOD! Go back to space 12.

21

20 19 18 17 16 15

Oh no! A pipe has burst. Slip back to space 6.

DETOUR

14

DETOUR

9 10 11 12 13

A new bridge has been built. Take it to space 29.

You've found a shortcut. Zoom off to space 20.

OBSTRUCTION

It's bad news when a road is blocked on a journey, but this maddening game
is all about blocking your opponent.

You need four coins or candies each (different colors for each player).

The rules are simple: take turns placing a counter anywhere on the grid
as long as there is a clear one-square space, above, below, beside, or
diagonally, between it and any other counter on the board.

The winner is the last person to play, as the other player has nowhere to
place their counter.

For example:

If the first player goes into the blue square,
the next player cannot put their counter in
any of the gray squares.

When the next player goes into the pink
square, even more squares are out of bounds.

Near the end, the
game might look like
this. It is pink's turn,
but blue will win,
because wherever pink
moves, there is still a
space for blue to make
the last move.

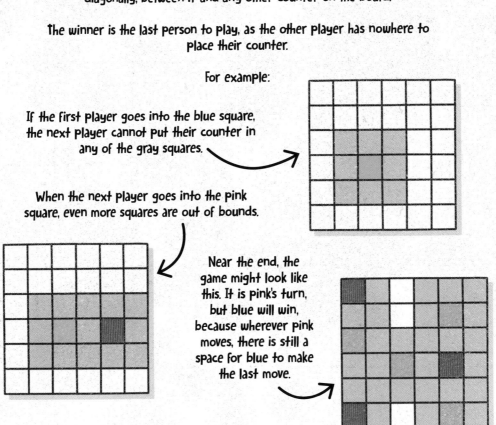

Of course, in real life the out-of-bounds squares are not helpfully
colored gray. You have to imagine the space around the counters.

LOTS OF LEGS

This game is most fun played in a car or bus.
The aim is to count as many legs as possible.

It's best to divide into two teams. One takes one side of the car and one takes the other side. All you have to do is count the number of legs you see on birds, animals, and people in pictures. Don't count real people or animals, or your numbers will be in the thousands in no time, but signs and pictures are fine.

If you see a restaurant called the White Horse, for example, with a horse on the sign outside, you can count four legs. If the horse has a rider, that would be six legs.

You can also see pictures in store windows and on signs, trucks, and billboards – in fact, all over the place. Some advertisements have lots of people or animals on them. You might be tempted to guess at hundreds. But remember, the same advertisement could easily appear on the other side.

The winner is the team with the most legs when you decide to stop counting.

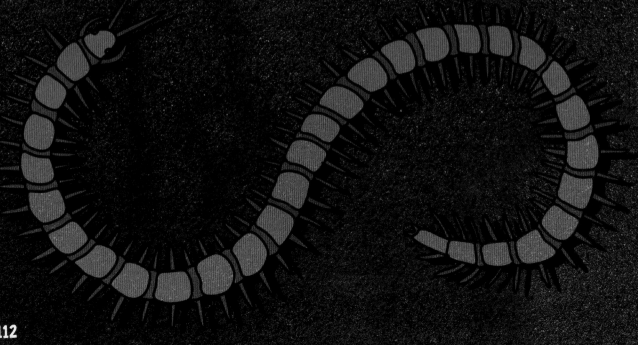

SLEEPWALK

If you need a nap but find it hard to nod off, try taking your sleepy finger for a stroll. Just look at the shape below and trace it slo-o-o-wly with your finger, letting all thoughts fade away. You'll soon find your eyes closing.

MAZE CHASE

Start on one side of the maze while your travel pal starts on the other. Whizz around the maze with one finger and see which of you is first to reach the single parking space in the center. Brrrm brrrm noises and screeching as you go around the corners is always a good idea!

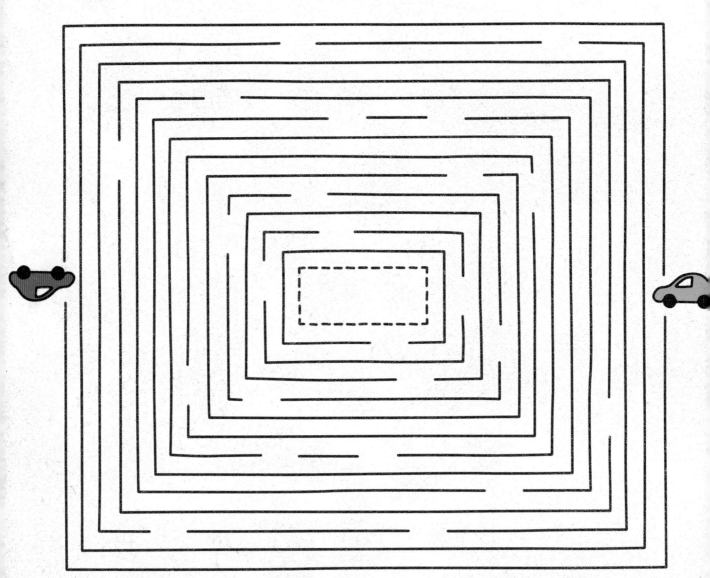

ANIMAL, VEGETABLE, MINERAL...

Here's a guessing game where you can choose anything in the whole world and ask your friends to guess it in 20 questions. All you have to do at the start is to say whether it is animal, vegetable, or mineral.

ANIMAL would include all birds, animals, fish, insects, spiders, reptiles and people, or anything made from them, such as leather, an omelet, a sausage, a pearl, or a sheepskin rug.

VEGETABLE would include any plants, from moss to trees, or anything made from them, such as paper, wood, baskets, bread, or straw.

MINERAL includes nonliving things that come from the Earth, or anything made from them, such as metals, coal, plastic, diamonds, stone, gasoline, clay, and glass.

The 20 questions can have only "yes" or "no" answers. The person who guesses what you are thinking of becomes the next chooser.

ELBOW SEMAPHORE

Signaling with flags was used at sea in the 1800s and is still sometimes done today. The signaler holds a flag in each hand and changes arm positions for each letter of the alphabet and other signals.

Trying to do this in a car, plane, or train would be madness. There just isn't room. Elbow semaphore uses the same idea but with hands instead of flags and with elbows clamped to your sides. So no one gets hurt ... except perhaps by laughing too much. Somehow elbow semaphore is hilarious, with the signaler looking like a cross between a puppet and a penguin.

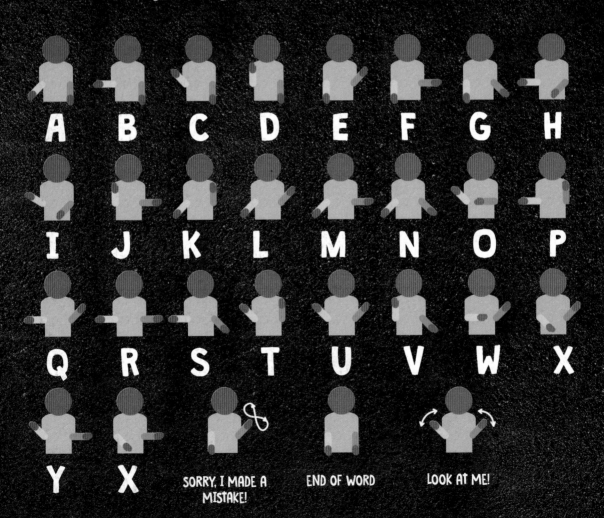

A B C D E F G H
I J K L M N O P
Q R S T U V W X
Y X   SORRY, I MADE A MISTAKE!   END OF WORD   LOOK AT ME!

SIGNALS SAY...

Can you figure out the names of these signalers? They are signaling their names in elbow semaphore. Check on page 127 to see if you are right. Then practice yourself. Remember to keep your hands flat and try not to giggle.

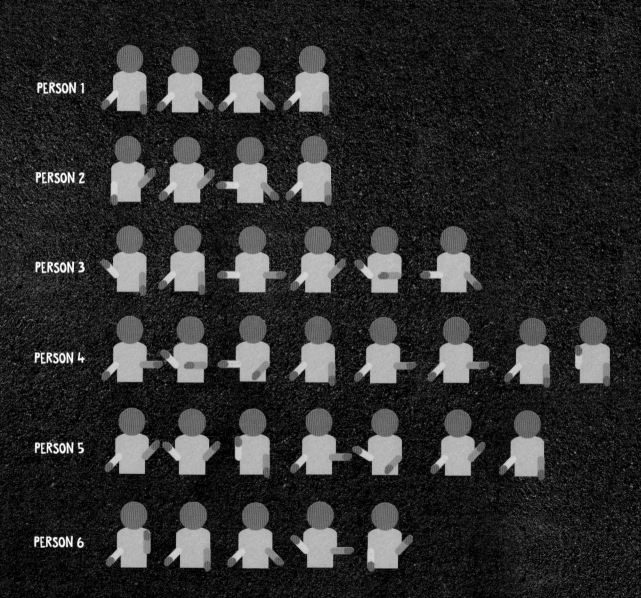

FOX AND GEESE

This game for two has been played for hundreds of years – but it's still fun today. Decide before you start if you want to be the fox or the geese.

You need 13 coins or pieces of candy to be the geese and a different coin, bottle top, or piece of candy to be the fox. Here's how you play:

1. Put the fox and geese on the board in this pattern. Each piece always sits on the corner of a square.

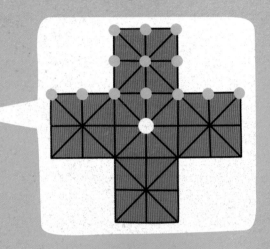

2. The geese always go first. At each turn, the player can move one goose to the next empty position. A goose can slide along any line, including diagonal ones. So, if a goose is in the position below, it can go to any of the arrow points as long as that point is empty.

3. The fox can also move one space at a time, but if it is next to a goose and there is a space beyond, the fox can jump over the goose and take it off the board, as in checkers (see page 20). If it can, the fox can keep jumping over geese and taking them off until it can't hop over another goose and has to stop. The fox doesn't HAVE to hop over a goose, even if it can. It can make a different move.

4. The geese win if they trap the fox so that it can't move. The fox wins if it takes off so many geese that they can't trap it.

119

A DOZEN PUZZLES

Don't let these teasers give you brain strain! All of them have sensible answers if you think about them a little bit. Turn to page 127 to check your answers.

1. If the day after the day before yesterday was Tuesday, and the day before the day after tomorrow is Thursday, what day is today?

2. Seven children huddle under one small umbrella. None of them gets wet. How come?

3. A man jumps out of a small airplane without a parachute. Amazingly, he survives and is not even hurt. How can that be?

4. What can you hold with your right hand but never with your left hand?

5. A girl threw a ball as hard as she could. There was nothing attached to it and it did not hit anything, but it turned and came back to her. How?

6. Is this boat sailing to the left or to the right?

7. A country has a railway line running from the east coast to the west coast. One train sets off from the west coast and another sets off from the east coast at exactly the same time, but the second train is traveling 10 miles (16 km) an hour faster than the first one. Which train will be closest to the west coast when they are passing each other?

8. A policeman saw a truck driver going the wrong way down a one-way street, but he didn't try to stop him. Why not?

9. A man on a trip set up his tent. Then he walked 1 mile (1.6 km) south, 1 mile (1.6 km) east, and 1 mile (1.6 km) north and found himself back at his tent. He was just about to go inside when a bear came along and ate him. What color was the bear?

10. How much soil is there in a round hole that is 3 feet (1 meter) deep and 9 feet (3 meters) across?

11. A traveler arrived in a strange town and asked if there was a barber, because he wanted to get his hair cut. It turned out there were two. The traveler went to check them out. The first barber had a messy shop and a terrible haircut himself. The second barber had a neat shop and a great haircut himself. Which one did the traveler go to?

12. A truck was taking much-needed food to a village struck by an earthquake. The only way to get there was through a tunnel in the mountains. But when the truck driver reached the tunnel, he realized his truck was 2 inches (5 cm) too tall and would not go through. How did he deliver the food?

THINK OF A NUMBER...

Best for journeys you haven't made before, this game can be played in cars, on trains, on planes, or even on foot. It's simple but addictive.

The game is to guess how many of something you will see on your trip. You can agree together on what you are looking for, or an adult can decide. Some things you could look for are:

how many bridges you go under
how many tunnels you go through
how many churches you see
how many babies are on your flight
how many people walk past your seat while you are moving along
how many cars beep at you
how many rivers you go over
how many police cars you see

Anything, in fact, can be part of the game. You can play one category at a time, or two, or three. Each person guesses a number. Be sure everyone knows when the game will stop. The winner is the person who guesses correctly most often.

PASSWORD

Sometimes frustrating, always fun, this is like charades without the acting.

This is a good game for two teams of two, each made up of one back-seat passenger and one front-seat traveler, who must not be allowed to look at this page.

The aim is to pass a word from the selection below from the back to the front. No acting or signaling is allowed, but knowing your partner well is a real advantage.

1. The back-seat passenger chooses one of the words below and gives a one-word clue.

2. The front-seat traveler makes a one-word guess. If they are right, the team scores 10 points. If not, the back-seat passenger gives another one-word clue. This time, the team wins 9 points if the guess is correct.

3. The "passer" has ten chances to pass the word, with the score going down each time. When the word is guessed correctly, or ten guesses have been made, the other back-seat/front-seat team has their turn, with a different word.

TREE   SHIRT   MARKET   BASKET

ORANGE   GUITAR   CUSHION   OSTRICH

BOOT   STREAM   ANGEL   BREAKFAST

TOE   PENGUIN   BLOOD   PUDDLE

PRINCESS   PRUNE   BUTTER   PAGE

GIANT   CORNER   STAMP   BLINK   KITE

CARROT   ENVELOPE   PATH

CANDY SOLITAIRE

Bored and on your own? This game is just for you. You will need 44 small pieces of candy. They can be different colors and shapes – and you can eat them as you play if you want, but make sure you don't get a stomachache!

1. Put the candies on the board so that each spot is covered but the center space is empty.

2. Your aim is to remove all the candies from the board except one, which should end up in the center space. You can move any candy you want each time but only by jumping over the piece next to it. This can be in any direction, but there must be an empty space for it to land on. The candy you jump over is taken off the board. (What you do with it then is up to you!) You can see that your first move will have to be to jump a piece into the center space because that's the only space that is empty.

3. Keep jumping and taking candies off the board until you have only one left, in the middle. It's not easy. To begin with, you will find that some candies get left behind. Keep practicing to see if you can figure out how to "rescue" all of them. If you can't, turn to page 128 and you'll see how to do it!

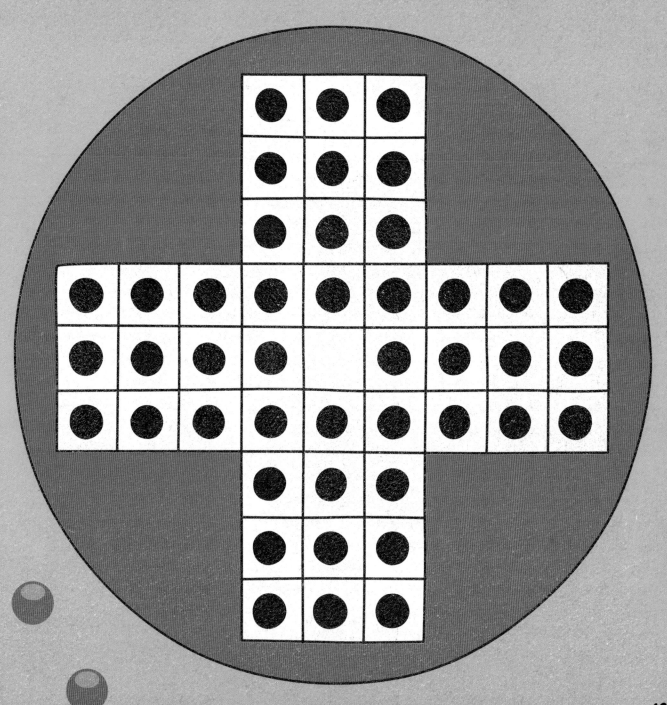

ANSWERS

Page 7: If you remembered six items, well done! Eight items, awesome! Ten items, you are a Master of Memory!

Page 10: Starting at the top and reading from left to right: TURKEY, NEW YORK, RUSSIA, LONDON, MEXICO, CHINA, TOKYO, SINGAPORE, BRAZIL, NEPAL, FRANCE, ANTARCTICA, GREENLAND, AUSTRALIA, EGYPT.

Page 11: There are 59 candies in the jar.

Page 13: From the top, the messages say: ARE WE THERE YET; COME TO MY PARTY ON MONDAY; MEET ME AT MIDNIGHT; WAS IT YOU WHO CALLED ME?; HELP IM SOOOOO BORED.

Page 16: There are 27 triangles. The easiest way to check is first to count all the single triangles, then all the triangles made up of four little triangles (remember, they may be upside down), then all the triangles made up of nine triangles, then all the triangles made up of 16 triangles.

Page 24: 1: There was a grandmother, a mother, and a daughter. The mother and the daughter were both daughters in the group. The grandmother and the mother were both mothers. But there were only three people. 2. Well, only one! The person speaking the poem is going to St. Ives, but "met" the man, wives, sacks, cats, and kittens, so it sounds as if they were coming towards him from St. Ives. 3: As a matter of fact, we don't know which day Ben arrived at the campsite. Friday was the name of his horse! 4: A postage stamp! It is stuck to the corner of a letter or a postcard and can travel almost anywhere in the world.

Page 25: 1: Neither! They are the same length. 2: It's square and the sides are straight. The pattern underneath tricks our eyes into thinking that they bend. 3. Neither, they're the same length. 4: The center circles are exactly the same size as each other. 5. They look as though they're slanting towards each other, but the lines are actually all parallel.

Page 26: The first rhythm is the theme from the William Tell Overture, by Rossini. The other is Old MacDonald's Farm!

Page 28: There are 51 butterflies.

Page 33: There are 50 rectangles.

Page 41: Key 25 doesn't have a twin.

Page 44: There are 47 balloons floating free, which means that the balloon-buyer has three left.

Page 60: There are 31 worms.

Page 61: Seoul is the capital missing from the word search.

Page 66: Remembering ten items is fantastic. Remembering 15 is genius. And if you remembered all 20, we want to know your secret technique!

Page 77: There are 40 squares altogether.

Page 82: The Pacific is missing. It's no wonder that the biggest ocean in the world wouldn't fit into a word search!

Page 90: Someone has claimed the blue button.

Page 117: The names of the signalers are Anna, Elsa, Carlos, Mohammad, Ludmila, and Kanye.

Page 120: 1. Today is Wednesday. 2. It isn't raining! 3. The airplane is still on the ground. 4. Your left hand! Anything else, you could hold with either hand. 5. She threw it straight up into the air above her head. Gravity brought it back down again! 6. Neither! It isn't moving at all! 7. As they are passing each other, they are both in the same place, so they are both the same distance from the west coast. 8. The truck driver was walking, not driving his truck. 9. The bear was white. In order to walk one mile (1.6 km) south, one mile (1.6 km) east, and one mile (1.6 km) north and still arrive back at his tent, the man must have pitched camp at the North Pole. This is because the Earth is a sphere and the North Pole sits right at the top of it. The only bears to be found there are polar bears, which are white. 10. None at all! A hole doesn't have any soil in it. 11. The traveler went to the barber with the bad haircut. He figured that the only way this barber could get his hair cut was by the other barber, who was a hopeless haircutter with a shop that was very neat and tidy because hardly anyone went there! 12. The driver took a little bit of air out of his tires – just enough to lower the truck by 2 inches (5 cm). As soon as he got through the tunnel, he could inflate his tires again.

ANSWERS

Page 124:

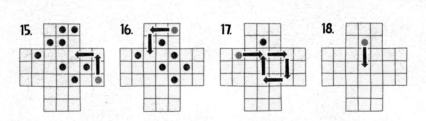